# Studies in
# British Society

Edited by J. A. BANKS

*The University of Liverpool*

ROUTLEDGE & KEGAN PAUL
*London*

*First published 1969*
*by Routledge & Kegan Paul Limited*
*Broadway House, 68–74 Carter Lane*
*London E.C.4*

*Printed in Great Britain*
*by Hazell Watson and Viney Limited*

© *Thomas Y. Crowell Company, 1968*

*SBN 7100 6382 2*

830476

*c*

# ❧ Contents

# ∾ Introduction

In his recent survey of the development of sociology since the turn of the century, the English sociologist John Madge did not include the work of any of his countrymen as the main subject of one of his chapters. He confessed that he would have liked to be able to do so but did not think that any justified inclusion in the story of the attempt to build a scientific sociology, in spite of other merits they might have. Indeed, apart from Emile Durkheim's classic study of suicide at the very beginning (1897), all the research discussed was conducted in the United States, almost wholly by sociologists who were American by origin or adoption. "If one thinks in terms of empirically based studies," he asserted, "the center of gravity today is undeniably in the United States. . . . Although this is not necessarily admitted by all Europeans, the American sociology of the last two or three decades is also the most productive not only of techniques but also of empirically tested ideas." [1]

This does not mean that contributions to scientific sociology have not been made elsewhere—some of them are referred to and reproduced in part in the present volume—but it does mean that American work has provided the impetus behind much of the research carried out in the rest of the world during this time. In spite of a long native tradition going back into the nineteenth century, or, as some would say, to the eighteenth at least, [2] current British sociological research has very little in common with the

[1] John Madge, *The Origins of Scientific Sociology* (London: Tavistock Publications, 1963), p. 2.
[2] Donald MacRae, "Great Britain," in Joseph Roucek, ed., *Contemporary Sociology* (London: Owen, 1959), pp. 699–700.

work of past sociologists. The one exception to this might possibly be historically based sociology, a field John Madge did not cover in his book, although even here the once dominant figure of L. T. Hobhouse has been of less significance than Max Weber as rediscovered by American sociologists. Hobhouse's evolutionary emphasis[3] went out of fashion soon after the Second World War for empirically oriented historical research into sociological issues; and the work of Sidney and Beatrice Webb,[4] which was not so emphatically evolutionary in structure, however much it was in spirit, has contributed more to social administration and to the formulation of social policy than it has to the development of a cumulative body of knowledge about how society actually works.

Therefore, in giving the appropriate sociological setting for the following selections from seven English studies, all published in the 1960's, reference must be made to the American rather than to the English work with which they have most affinity. Thus, Margaret Stacey's survey of Banbury, *Tradition and Change,* carries echoes of Lloyd Warner's Yankee City series; *Coal and Conflict* by W. H. Scott and his colleagues has the undertones of a running debate with Elton Mayo and the Human Relations School of industrial sociology; Bryan Wilson's *Sects and Society* more closely resembles Liston Pope's *Millhands and Preachers* than any English work; *Pentonville* by Terence and Pauline Morris owes much to Gresham Sykes's *Society of Captives*; Ostergaard and Halsey's *Power in Co-operatives* openly acknowledges its debt to Seymour Lipset's *Union Democracy*; and the Newsons' *Infant Care in an Urban Community* is set in the tradition of family studies inspired by Margaret Mead. The three longitudinal studies by J. W. B. Douglas, of which an extract from the last only is included below, cannot be so easily placed in this way, but this is mainly because

[3] J. A. Hobson and Morris Ginsberg, *L. T. Hobhouse: His Life and Work* (London: Allen and Unwin, 1931). Harry Elmer Barnes, ed., "Leonard Trelawney Hobhouse," *An Introduction to the History of Sociology* (Chicago: University of Chicago Press, 1948), ch. 32.
[4] T. S. Simey, "The Contribution of Sidney and Beatrice Webb to Sociology," *The British Journal of Sociology,* XII (June, 1961), 106–230.

they have their origin in a rather different tradition—that of demographic sociology which has had a continuous history of its own from at least the time of Malthus [5] and which also in the United States has remained to some extent aloof from the separate trend of sociological research and theory, in spite of the fact that the majority of demographic courses there are more frequently offered in sociology departments than elsewhere.[6]

Perhaps it should be emphasized that this American influence on English sociological research has been felt, not on the pursuit of empirical data as such, but in terms of the context in which it has been collected and presented. The history of social surveys in Britain is a long one, going back through the publications of the Manchester and London statistical societies to the establishment of the Royal Society in 1662. These provided a wealth of information, often obtained at firsthand, about the condition of the working classes and the associated problems of poverty, illiteracy, overcrowding, and disease. But excellent though so many of these surveys are, they are not sociological as this term is understood today. Nor were they related to the main stream of sociological reasoning, stemming from Auguste Comte and Herbert Spencer, through Emile Durkheim and Max Weber, to the highly sophisticated theory builders of the present day. If it is accepted, as the editor of the first volumes in this series put it, "that there exists an order of things in nature and, more specifically, that the behavior of human beings, like other natural phenomena, shows regular and recurrent patterns" and that "the proper method of discovering and accounting for these patterns" is scientific procedure,[7] then British empirical surveys have been strong on discovering isolated facts rather than patterns and weak in attempting to account for what they discovered. They are still worthy of attention as sources for any historically minded

[5] Frank Lorimer, "The Development of Demography," in Philip M. Hauser and Otis D. Duncan, eds., *The Study of Population* (Chicago: University of Chicago Press, 1959), pp. 140 *et seq.*

[6] W. E. Moore, "Sociology and Demography," in *ibid.*, p. 832.

[7] Derek L. Phillips, ed., *Studies in American Society: I* (New York: Thomas Y. Crowell, 1965), p. 2.

sociologist who seeks data to test a hypothesis, but they themselves make no contribution to such forms of knowledge. Where explanations have been offered at all they have been fabricated post hoc, and the only kinds of ideas they were explicitly formulated to falsify have been simple assertions of the all-or-none, more-or-less variety, such as the extent of poverty among the working classes in an urban area.[8]

In contrast to this lack of a sociological perspective, the seven studies in this book are rich in their sociological content or implications. Their choice, in the first instance, was determined by this consideration rather than by the nature of the facts about English society which each of them has been diligent to collect and reproduce. Nevertheless, concern has also been exercised to select those studies which exemplify major areas of importance in contemporary English life, at least insofar as the editor has been able to distinguish between what is important and what is not. This may well mean that other sociological works, worthy of inclusion in a larger volume, have been left out and not even perhaps mentioned in the reading lists. The mere omission of a study should however not be assumed to imply that the editor has thought poorly of it; it should rather be understood as a consequence of his own limitations, both in the selection of themes as important and in the choice of studies to illuminate them. The editor makes haste to affirm that he believes the seven books he has chosen to be among those most British academic sociologists have used regularly in their teaching and in discussing research topics at conferences in recent years.

The first of the studies from which a selection has been made is concerned with the impact of new industry upon the social life and social stratification system of an old English town. Banbury is a characteristically English mixture of the old and the new, where the new consists of "immigrants" of the same ethnic origin as the old, however much in other ways they are culturally different.

[8] T. S. Simey and M. B. Simey, *Charles Booth, Social Scientist* (London: Oxford University Press, 1960), p. 184.

*Tradition and Change* accordingly touches on an enduring feature of English society, persistent conflict between what has been and what is, focused, as is so often the case, on the differences between the social classes and the resistance to the erosion of social distances hallowed by custom. *Coal and Conflict,* the next study, is also concerned with change, but here the new is a form of organization, the nationalized industry, with its comprehensive scheme of collective negotiations and bargaining, developed to meet new conditions of employment. One of the political justifications for such a governmental measure was as a remedy for the poor morale of the coal industry in the interwar years. In sociological terms, W. H. Scott and his colleagues examined the roots of morale and conflict in the industry after nationalization and sought to explain what they found by reference to the situation and perspectives of the different occupational groups they studied.

The third selection in the book picks up this theme of the relation between situation and perspective, although in this case the key factor is not occupational differentiation but underprivilege and relative privilege. Bryan Wilson's *Sects and Society* explores the ideologies and social philosophies of two religious groups recruiting from the poor, the socially neglected, and the culturally deprived, and one from the established middle and the aspiring lower middle classes. By contrast, *Power in Co-operatives* returns to the study of a single organization, controlled and operated by representatives of the upper working class. The theme here is the classic one of Michels' iron law of oligarchy, or the difficulty of maintaining democratic participation in a social system when survival and efficiency demand special knowledge and abilities not widely dispersed throughout the population.

A prison does not have much in common with a cooperative society which people join voluntarily and which is intended to be democratically controlled. The sociological study of a London prison, indeed, is included to indicate how only rudimentary cooperation is possible in the compulsory association of a society of captives. *Pentonville* demonstrates how, in its own words, "in the maximum security prison all men are prisoners." The sixth reading, *The Home and the School,* turns to consider the selective procedures whereby ability in English society is directed to where educational opportunities are greatest, emphasizing social class differences in these respects, just as John and Elizabeth Newson emphasize such differences in the treatment of very young children in their *Infant Care in an Urban Community.* Thus, in many respects the studies link with one another, covering the urban scene, industry, religion, political behavior, the family and socialization, while at the same time touching upon issues of current political and social debate in English life.

As in the books edited by Derek L. Phillips, each selection appears exactly as in the parent volume except in the following respects: (1) certain passages and footnotes of secondary importance are omitted when such omission does not seriously impair the utility of the selection; (2) a simple phrase or sentence is occasionally inserted to effect a suitable transition when material has been omitted or when a brief explanation of unfamiliar material is necessary; and (3) footnotes and tables are renumbered.

Each selection is preceded by a brief introduction which refers among other things to the methods of investigation employed, and it is followed by a short list of other writings intended to lead the student to a more comprehensive knowledge of the area covered. The aim, of course, is to stimulate the student to read the whole book from which the extract is taken, as a preliminary to the serious study of sociology, preferably on a comparative basis. In this sense the collection may be of more value to the American student than to the native Englishman, since it is hoped that it will introduce him, perhaps for the first time, to a not-inconsequential, growing body of sociological research of some relevance. At the same time the English student may come to see the work of his countrymen in a new light, and the dual purpose of this selection will be thus achieved.

# ✍Tradition and Change

MARGARET STACEY

*This is a study of what happens when new industry moves into an old country town and requires it to absorb thousands of immigrants. Banbury, a market center in the heart of England with some small industries, increased in size at about the same rate as the rest of the country for the first three quarters of the nineteenth century. It then dropped rapidly behind until by 1931 the population was not much larger than it had been in 1891. In 1933, however, an aluminum factory started production in the town, a corset factory was established, and the cattle, sheep, and horse markets were moved from the main streets. Over the next twenty years the population of Banbury increased by 35 percent, from about 13,000 inhabitants to about 19,000. Many of the immigrants came from great industrial cities in the Midlands and the North, with the result that a new way of life was superimposed on the deep-rooted traditionalism of the original inhabitants. The following pages, taken from a chapter on the social class and social status characteristics of the population, demonstrate how this produced a town divided vertically between traditionalists and nontraditionalists and horizontally between the middle and the working classes.*

*Mrs. Stacey and her colleagues spent three years in Banbury,*

SOURCE: Margaret Stacey, *Tradition and Change: A Study of Banbury,* Chapter 8 (pp. 144–64). Copyright © 1960 by the Oxford University Press. Reprinted by permission of the Clarendon Press, Oxford.

*participating in the life of the town, analyzing its public records, and talking to the leading members of the community and of the organizations centered there. They also carried out a questionnaire inquiry, interviewing a sample of households to determine the composition of the family and the religious and political affiliations of its members. This sample was obtained by selecting every fifth address on the register of electors, and information was collected about all the individuals living at each address. Homes rather than individuals were chosen because the research team wanted information about households and families, as well as about individuals. Altogether 935 homes, covering 1,015 households and 3,387 individuals, representing about 18 percent of the total population, participated in the inquiry.*

Tradition and Change *may be criticized for not making as much use of the opportunity of a schedule inquiry as might have been expected. When it was conducted in July, 1950, there had been no official census in Britain for nearly twenty years, and because it was designed to fill in that gap in information, it therefore concentrated on the kind of objective data such a census would normally have provided; and the research team relied, for its analysis of social class and traditionalism, upon observations made by its members over the whole period of time that they lived in Banbury and upon many other minor inquiries they conducted in the town. The strength of the study, in any case, rests upon a feature of the town which has been widely recognized since it was published, namely that it is a meeting point of at least two cultures, the local and the national. It is for this that it has been praised as a sensitive appraisal of a phenomenon characteristic of much of Britain at this time. In this sense, Banbury approximates a microcosm of urban life in a changing community where traditional values are still very strong, a feature of Britain which has so often been remarked upon by visitors to this country since the end of the Second World War.*

*Keeping in mind that the research findings have been derived from the accumulation of data through the employment of a number*

8

*of techniques, one can read Mrs. Stacey's study for both its descrip-*
*tive and its analytical content.*

It is not possible to construct for Banbury and district a simple
*n*-fold class system. That is to say, the total population cannot be
placed in a series of horizontal groupings, members of each group
being assumed to have parity with each other and able to recognize
each other as social equals if they should meet. Nor is it possible to
place people upon one social status scale, ranked on a basis of commonly agreed social characteristics. There is a reasonably clear-cut
status system within the traditional society, linked with the traditional class system. Among non-traditionalists there are numbers of
status groups based most often on occupational status, but on a variety
of occupational hierarchies rather than on one single system. Prediction about the class and status position of a traditionalist may be
fairly accurate; only the roughest prediction is possible for the non-
traditionalist. Some very broad equivalence between traditionalists
and non-traditionalists on a three-fold system can be seen at a fairly
high level of abstraction.

These conclusions, which are described and justified below, were
reached by participation in the life of the town at all levels and by
observation of who associated socially with whom in both formal
and informal groups. The study of formal associations provided a
valuable guide for those in the middle ranges, but informal associations were not neglected here and assumed greater importance for
those who do not take much part in formal associations. The bridge
sets, sherry parties, and tea parties, the 'regulars' at pubs and hotels,
and associations among neighbours, are examples of the informal
groups observed.

Direct questioning about social class was almost confined to
members of the adult tutorial class which was associated with the
survey. Its results largely served to show that the indirect method of
observation was likely to be the most satisfactory.

[Sociological research] . . . has shown that probably everybody

9

has a working 'construct' of the social class system based upon their own experiences and aspirations, a construct which may or may not fit the facts of the social structure as seen by the sociologist. Moreover, status groups are so complex and confusing that they may be pressed into almost any conceptual framework. These two facts affect the social theorist, the field-worker, and the layman alike.

At first the adult students produced as many different class systems as there were students. This was before the subject had been treated in lectures. After the six-fold classification used by Warner had been explained to them, almost all concluded that such a system also applied to Banbury! After all, it was neat, they had all heard of upper, middle, and lower classes (although they said 'working' not 'lower') and they were prepared to accept sub-divisions they had not thought of in the large areas of society of which they had not direct knowledge. Further theoretical discussion led to further amendment of the students' concepts.

In any case, direct questioning about social class, both inside the adult class and outside it, met an initial reticence that amounted to a taboo. The reasons for this reticence are connected with the class system itself and with the changes that are taking place within it. There are certain social rules which say that the existence of status and class differences should be assumed but not spoken about. One effect of this is to make people pretend, to themselves as well as to others, that the differences do not exist or are less pervasive than is in fact the case. It is the existence of these rules which in part makes the class system workable. It is 'not done' to 'set yourself up' or 'write the other man down' although it is done every day by implication and sometimes remarkably directly. An example of this attitude came from a Colonel's wife speaking to a new-comer to a village on whom she had called. 'I think you'll like the X's,' she said, 'and then there are the Y's and the Z's; otherwise I don't think there is anybody. But of course it's bad luck for you there are no children in the village.' (The new-comer had a young family.) Happily this startling picture of rural depopulation was contradicted by statistics which showed that the village had a population of about 500 with a normal complement of children. Yet this woman, who referred to 98 per cent. of her fellow villagers as 'nobody', as people you would not 'know', although in fact she knew a great many through the Women's Institute, saw no contradiction in saying: 'I shouldn't mind the socialists so much if they didn't bring class into everything.' Her real complaint was, of course, that the socialists, instead of taking class for granted, talk about class and, worse still, question it.

Reticence which springs from this taboo is increased because class is associated with politics, itself a taboo subject except among intimates and those of known common allegiance. In consequence, even those who accept the rightness of the traditional class system tend to be self-conscious about it and feel that perhaps 'it's not quite democratic'. This attitude leads to the self-justifying 'well, anyway, we're all workers nowadays'. It may even lead to a denial of obvious fact. One informant, for example, denied that one of the most exclusive clubs in town was in fact exclusive at all. 'Oh no,' she said, 'nowadays anyone can join.' The club's constitution may not formally bar anyone, but analysis showed that in practice by no means 'anyone' joined.

Given time these difficulties could be, and were, overcome among friendly informants. But, added to the reticence which springs from the social taboos, there is honest confusion about the status system in Banbury. Banbury is no longer a place where 'you know where you are' as, according to informants, it used to be. It was a society, apparently, in which the status of individuals and their families, indeed of individuals as members of their families, was clearly understood. Now a great many immigrants and the unfamiliar hierarchy of a large factory have been added. For example, the people of Banbury find it difficult to place a man such as a department head who is employed (a sign of low status) and yet has more power (a sign of high status) than many in the town who are their own masters; or again, a metallurgist, a skill previously unknown in the town, who appears to have little or no authority (low status) and yet has a university education (very high status). The confusion is increased because people of this sort are usually immigrants whose family background is unknown and many of whose associations are outside the district. Nobody knows where to put them and, in fact, they cannot be 'put' into the traditional status system of Banbury, it has no place for them. Some individuals have worked their way in, many others have not and are not concerned to do so.

To have built up a picture of the status system in Banbury from information given by townspeople about their 'sets' would have been a difficult task. Lengthy interviews would have been necessary to break down initial resistance. Added to this are the dangers of reification and the partial and confused nature of individual knowledge, for outside the traditional system the status system is fragmentary. A very great many people would therefore have had to be interviewed if all levels of the town were to be adequately covered. Such large-scale intensive interviewing was beyond the resources available.

The methods of observation and participation used have produced results which can be described but which have not been precisely measured. For the class structure revealed by the evidence collected was in many ways different from what had been expected: the impossibility, for example, of placing everybody, even broadly, in one class system had not been suspected at the outset. Statistical data, measuring objective status characteristics, was collected on the assumption of a unitary system. Consequently only partial measurement of the groups finally identified and described below is possible. The author prefers, however, to describe groups which have been seen to exist rather than to classify people on an objective characteristic, thus apparently identifying and measuring a group, although it has not been observed in operation.

Since social class, where it exists, is, by definition, an open system (as opposed to a closed caste system, for example) there are no hard and fast lines between classes. Rather there are a great many status grades which shade off imperceptibly into each other. Each status grade has observable social characteristics and associated attitudes which differentiate it from its neighbours.

For the traditional area these status grades can be validly

grouped together, on the basis of certain shared characteristics, into three classes. Such a threefold system is not uncommonly used, although few studies make any clear differentiation between upper and middle classes. Indeed, most studies of social class hitherto made in this country have tended to pay little attention to the upper class. It is, after all, a numerically small group and studies involving social class have tended to be made in places where the upper class do not live. In the context of Banbury and district it was impossible to ignore the existence of upper-class people. Furthermore, in so far as this class sets the standards and the aspirations of traditional social class attitudes, if only indirectly below the level of its frontier with the middle class, it is important out of all proportion to its size.

In the present study the dividing line between classes has been drawn at the points where the social characteristics of the status groups show the most fundamental changes. That is to say, members of the class above have characteristics which it is difficult or impossible to acquire in an adult lifetime. But, because the system is continuous, there are in each case status groups on the frontiers between the classes, which partake of the characteristics and the values of the class above and the class below them. Therefore they cannot be allocated to one class or the other.

It is easier to move up within a class than between classes, except for those who start on the frontier between classes. In practice, in terms of face-to-face relationships, belonging to a class (or moving up or down) involves being accepted in a 'set' which has a status in a wider context. The context may be different from but not unassociated with the class allocation people give themselves in relation to the country as a whole and to their political-interest class, e.g. 'middle class' or 'worker'. The techniques of acceptance or rejection are subtle. You must possess appropriate characteristics: occupation, home, residence area, income (suitably spent), manners, and attitudes. You must know or learn the language and the current private 'passwords' of the group. You must be introduced. If you fail in these particulars you will simply be 'not known'. Nothing is said or done. The barrier is one of silence. This is also true for those who are dropped for some offence against the code of their class; they may never discover what their alleged offence is and certainly have no chance of defence. They simply find that invitations cease and backs are turned at the bar. In the working class rejection may be as silent or it may be more open; open mockery, for example, of language that is too 'haw-haw'.

For social status, and to that extent social class, involves a totality of status differences: no one characteristic is an adequate index to it. The prime essentials of social class are the manner of life a man leads and the people he associates with on a basis of equality. In social class home and working life meet and the roles of husband and wife are both important: how much money he provides and how she spends it; where and what sort of house he provides and how she runs it; if he is to be acceptable to a group of people so must she be. For social status is a family rather than a purely individual matter. Factors like occupation and income are important because they determine the manner of life that is possible: size and equipment of house, furnishings, dress, hospitality, and so on, hours of work and amount of leisure time. The status carried by the occupation itself plays some determining role in social class but is not necessarily paramount.

But these factors are by no means the only ones. People may choose to live differently from the way in which their income and occupation status would lead one to expect. Cases of people who were living according to the customs, the values, and attitudes of a grade 'above' or 'below' them (in terms of their income and occupation position), and who were accepted by the grade of their choice, were found at three different social status levels. Examples were also found of people who have failed to be accepted by their 'economic' peers and who therefore had a lower status than expected.

Moreover, factors which are not purely social can come in. Attention was focused during the field-work on social rather than psychological factors, but it was noticed that personality was often the explanation for individuals who were 'misplaced' in terms of their class; individuals who, while apparently lacking certain essential social qualifications, had 'got in' to a superior group or who, with the qualifications, were nevertheless out-grouped.

For social class is judged in practice by the impression produced by the sum total of status-giving characteristics. The qualifying 'tests' for admission to a status group may be passed by those who possess most but not all of a given set of characteristics. That is why individuals are found who associate not merely in a different status group from what one might expect, judged on the basis of 'objective' characteristics alone, but even in a different class.

The table below shows the main outlines of the social class and status system for Banbury and district (the class system in the rural area was not observed below the level of the gentry and the large farmers). It should be pointed out that this represents a considerable abstraction in the sense that it is not the way any one person in the town thinks of it. Furthermore, the characteristics given are those possessed by an 'ideal type' at the centre of the group. Not everyone in the group necessarily possesses all of them.

Traditional and non-traditional status groups have been separated. The former fall into a fairly clear class system which the latter do not. Equivalences are suggested between the two sides of the table on the basis of known associations on terms of equality between traditionalists and non-traditionalists. It will be seen that they range fairly widely, showing both the lack of system among the non-traditionalists and the fluidity of the total situation.

In the traditional class system the three classes identified have been called upper, middle, and working. The single most important characteristic which divides the upper from the middle class is one of education. Members of the traditional upper class in the Banbury district were all educated at one of the major public schools.[1]

---

[1] While the precise definition of a 'public school' is difficult and membership of the Headmasters' Conference certainly too broad for use here, the upper class regard about two dozen as 'good' public schools and most of the aristocracy patronize two or three of these. The Banbury and district telephone directory shows a total of 92 men and women in the district who bear titles, senior rank in the services (Colonel or over), or who live in a house called 'hall', 'park', &c., with the village name as prefix. 24 are in the last category,

In contrast, a common educational background is by no means a characteristic of the Banbury middle class. Its members were not educated at public schools in the upper-class definition, although some went to minor public schools. A number were educated at private schools, others at local grammar schools, and others again received only an elementary education. Education, therefore, does not necessarily provide a distinction between the middle class and the working class, although it is true that the majority of the working class have received only an elementary education while a much higher proportion of the middle class received a secondary education. The single most important characteristic which divides the middle class from the working class is occupation. The middle class are either employed non-manual workers with some power and responsibility or are proprietors. The working class are manual workers, but not necessarily without responsibility over others.

Two status groups have been identified in the upper class: 'county' and 'gentry'. The 'county' is headed by the few aristocrats who live in the district. The aristocracy, nationally, is drawn from nobles who have inherited their titles; it is an informal social group and one which forms the centre of the court circle; the crown is its head. For the rest, the 'county' includes retired senior officers from the services and some landed gentry (often younger sons of aristocrats or in some way related), provided that they play an active part in the affairs of the district or in one of the hunts. The 'gentry' is composed of men and women from the same sort of families and with the same sort of education as the 'county' who, either from choice, because they are retired or widowed, or from lack of means, participate in public life on a reduced scale.

---

39 hold senior rank in the services, 29 bear titles. 21 of the total of 92 are women. Of the 71 men, 36 are in *Who's Who;* 26 of these are shown as having been educated at one of nine major English public schools (16 at Eton); 3 at Scots or Irish public schools, and 3 privately; the remaining 4 gave no particulars. Apart from any who are members of the non-traditional upper class, an analysis of the remaining 34 who are not listed in *Who's Who* would probably give a broadly similar result. The majority passed from public school to Sandhurst, Oxford, or Cambridge. None went to a 'provincial' university.

Social Class and Social Status Groups

| | TRADITIONAL CLASS SYSTEM | | | | NON-TRADITIONAL STATUS GROUPS | Reference to Traditional Status groups |
|---|---|---|---|---|---|---|
| | | STATUS GROUP | | | | |
| CLASS | RURAL | TOWN | | | | |
| UPPER | 1 COUNTY | | 1 | | Industrial Upper | 1–3 |
| | 2 GENTRY | | 2 | | Banbury Senior Directors and Managers | 2–4 |
| | 3 ══ UPPER FRONTIER ══ | | 3 | | Newer Professions | |
| MIDDLE | 4 | MIDDLE | 4 | | Industrial Technicians and Staffs | 4–6 |
| | 5 ══ LOWER FRONTIER ══ | | 5 | | Respectable | 6 |
| | 6 | RESPECTABLE | 6 | | Ordinary | 7 |
| WORKING | 7 | ORDINARY | 7 | | Rough | 8 |
| | 8 | ROUGH | | | | |

The 'upper frontier' group lies between the middle and upper classes. The majority of its members had the same sort of education as the upper class; their manner of life and their attitudes are in many ways similar. But they 'work for a living' (many are in the older professions) as servants of the upper class and of other classes. Their personal associates are drawn partly from the upper class, where their educational background makes them acceptable, and partly from the middle class.

This 'upper frontier' group is perhaps nationally most often called 'upper-middle', but since in Banbury some of its members associate on terms of ease with some members of the gentry who are definitely upper class (as well as with middle-class people), this title has been avoided. Further, the rather loose, common use of 'upper-middle' also covers groups of professional and business men who do not share the upper-class characteristics so typical of the Banbury 'upper frontier'.[2]

Below the 'upper frontier' comes a status group 'middle' which is the centre of the middle class. There are a number of interest groups within it, the divisions into Anglican, Free Church, and Roman Catholic being perhaps the most important. It is the group from which the traditional political leaders in the town are drawn and also its social leaders. . . . The tradesmen and the businessmen of the town form the backbone of this group.

The 'lower frontier' group lies between the middle class and the working class. . . . In the same way that the 'upper frontier' is divided in characteristics and associations between the upper and the middle classes, so are members of the 'lower frontier' status group divided between the middle and working classes. Its mem-

[2] It is an apposite comment on occupation as an index of status that the social class of doctors (of the same medical rank) varies from one part of the country to another, from middle class to upper class, including the 'frontier' cases. It may be relevant to their status in Banbury, where they mostly fall in the upper frontier group, that there it is possible for general practitioners to live in, or almost in, the country, a characteristic piece of upper-class behaviour. Those, therefore, who appreciate the rural life are likely to self-select themselves to areas like Banbury.

bers include both manual and non-manual workers; among non-manual workers it includes both those who work on their own account and employed office workers; among manual workers it includes skilled men working on their own account and employed skilled workers. This group might be called 'lower-middle class', but equally some of its members might be called 'superior working class'; it is, in fact, a frontier group and has therefore been so named.

The working class itself is composed chiefly, but not exclusively, of manual workers (some are routine non-manual workers, for example) and does not include all manual workers. It has been divided into three status groups: 'respectable', 'ordinary', and 'rough'. This division has some relation to amount of skill and income, but the actual ranking for a family is made not on the basis of these factors alone, but on steadiness at work and excellence of housekeeping in addition. The 'rough' are identified by their failure to conform to these standards, by a failure to be 'clean and decent'; they are families where father is not regularly employed, where the house and children are not kept clean, and whose members are 'in trouble' with the police from time to time.

. . . . .

One of the effects of the objective class characteristics in combination is that as social status increases so does scale of living: houses not only increase in size and amenities, but are found farther and farther away from the town centre. All members of the upper class live right outside Banbury Borough in the rural area of the district; the middle class live in villages which neighbour the town or on the higher land to the south and west of the Borough. The working class live either in the crowded town centre or in the council estates on the outskirts, government action having upset what would otherwise have been a neat ecological map. It is still probably true that more of the traditional working class live in the town centre, many of those in the council estates on the outskirts being non-traditional workers, but the correlation is far from perfect. This geographic distance, of course, emphasizes the social distance between the classes and is commonly found in any 'class' society of this sort.

But this is by no means the whole story of the relationship between social class and geography; the size of the geographic area within which relationships at the face-to-face level are maintained also increases with social status. The basis of the upper-class social circle is national, with the west end of London as its 'town centre', *The Times* as its local paper, and certain national events, e.g. Ascot, as its focal points. It is a social circle whose members may have international connexions. It is remarkable of the upper class that they have practically no contact with Banbury itself; any contact they may have is limited to acts of patronage, presidencies of Banbury associations for example. Nor are immediate neighbours of any account in the upper class: a neighbour is a member of the same class within a radius of about thirty miles.

This wide basis for the face-to-face group is possible because members of the upper class can command the physical means of communication; they own cars and have telephones. So do many members of the middle class in Banbury and district, but they use their cars principally for business, for occasional journeys connected with the activities of their voluntary associations, and for holiday travel. If it could be measured, the proportion of their local to trunk calls would be found to be much higher than that of the upper class. For Banbury is the basis of the friendship circle in the middle class. Its members have friends outside Banbury, but are unconnected with any nationally based social group (a number of their voluntary organizations are nationally organized, however). They have some relationships with their next-door neighbours, but, their social circle is principally drawn from members of their own class with like interests to themselves living in the town or nearby villages.

The geographic horizon of the working class is more restricted again. The majority form their most important friendship groups in the street where they live and often within a part only of that street. The men have friends at work, but these are rarely leisure-time associates even when they live nearby. Nor do many members of this class take an active part in voluntary associations. The pub they go to is at the end of the street or just round the corner.

In another sense, also, a wider area of communication is possible for those of higher status, for command of language increases with social class. In the upper class not only is the command of written and spoken English high, but the common manner of speech given by the public schools is a class mark, and one which it is difficult (some say impossible) to acquire in adulthood. Middle-class command of language is reasonably good, but some solecisms are common and the accent of place of origin may usually be detected, for here speech is less standardized than in the upper class. Working-class command of language is less great, grammar tends to be inaccurate, and the accent an idiom of place of origin marked; vocabulary is more limited and less ability to deal with abstract ideas is shown. When members of the traditional working class belong to voluntary associations, they commonly excuse themselves from office on such grounds as 'I'm not handy with my pen'.

The factor which nowadays does not correlate steadily with class in Banbury, as elsewhere in England, is income and/or wealth, although the lowest incomes tend to be found at the bottom and the most wealth at the top. The way in which income is obtained does still vary reasonably consistently with class in the traditional system. Independent means and profits and fees in the upper class, profits and fees or salary and sometimes independent means in the middle class, and wages in the working class. Nowadays in Banbury a number of middle-class people are wealthier than some of the gentry (whose 'independent means' produce for them in some cases less than the wage of a skilled manual worker). Some workers, furthermore, earn more than some members of the middle class.

Although this is the case, it does not lead the possessors of these relatively high incomes to adopt the manner of life of the class above. Wealthy middle-class people in Banbury do not have nannies or send their children to major public schools; it would be out of class pattern and they do not wish, apparently, to attempt to change their class. Rather they live up to the highest standards set for the

Banbury middle class. Similarly, the better-off workers do not adopt the middle-class pattern, they live more lavishly on the working-class scale: they eat well, drink and smoke more, have TV sets, and new outfits for the wife and children for every public holiday. But they do not move from the rent-controlled or Council house and buy an owner-occupied house on a mortgage (which would be uneconomic for them but necessary if they wished to move into the middle class), nor do they join voluntary associations which are essentially middle class, nor send their children to private schools.

The evidence from Banbury is that the goals of the classes are different and that although income may not correlate with class, the way that income is spent does correlate with it; a choice is made on the basis of the values set by the class. Those who wish to raise their status aspire to the standards of a 'set' in the status group immediately above them, not to those of the class above them. Similarly, those whose means are reduced do not in consequence adopt the life of the class below, but live on a smaller scale within the values of the class to which they were brought up.

An attitude which is common to people in all classes within the traditional system is acceptance of loyalty to established institutions. Loyalty to the crown in the person of the monarch as a symbol of national unity is one example. Hence the importance to the traditional system of the aristocracy, leaders of the upper class, numerically few though they are. Traditionalists in Banbury and district accord status to the upper class by asking them to patronize their associations, although it is doubtful how clear they may be about distinctions between traditional and non-traditional members of the upper class, except for those few aristocratic families who have had associations with Banbury and district for many centuries. Loyalty to established institutions is also connected with conservatism in politics, or with anti-socialism. . . .

A loyalty to the traditional class system, or to its values, is also common to people who remain within it. Although touching the cap or curtseying to the squire and his lady have passed out of custom within living memory in Banbury district, all agree that 'There'll always be classes, stands to reason' and stress the importance of 'breeding', i.e. the inherited basis of social class. The ideals of the gentleman and 'gentlemanly' and 'ladylike' behaviour are found in all classes, although the interpretations of each differ from one class to another. Furthermore, the right to lead of those in a higher class, or in a higher status group within a class, is accepted. It is a right to lead, or a duty to follow, which is given by social position, a position which pervades many aspects of life. Traditionally, members of the upper class have positions of directorial power and responsibility and assume and are granted leadership roles at the national level outside the purely economic field. The middle class in the town have power and responsibility over others or at least freedom from masters. In the life of the town they assume leadership roles outside the economic field (but do not aspire to leadership, economic or other, at national level). The traditional working class (fewer of whom are found nowadays) work for masters and follow where they lead.

The traditional class system is therefore in many senses a total system: status in one field giving status in another. It rests upon the principle of social inheritance, children of families in each class being differently trained both formally and informally to fit their status.

But the number of people in Banbury and district who do not fit the traditional system is increasing. They include those who have positions they have not inherited, those who have moved up by new routes (State-aided education for example), those who have high status in one sphere and low in another. There are persons with considerable power, authority, and wealth whose family backgrounds the gentry 'don't know'. There are occupations that cannot be placed and there are ways of life and attitudes alien to the traditional class system.

People with these characteristics are non-traditionalists. They do not have a class system of their own. It is typical of non-traditionalism in Banbury that it is not a unity: the only factor which non-traditionalists have in common is non-conformity in some respect to the traditions of Banbury. Non-traditionalists of whatever status in Banbury are essentially without class in the traditional sense because they have not inherited an established position in an established system. Many of them are immigrants.

No recently ennobled working-class peers live in Banbury district, but there are those who have recently risen in rank, although from less lowly origins. They fail to fit into the traditional upper class not only because of family background and schooling, but also because their attitudes and interests differ from those of the traditionalist. Not only may the wealth of these non-traditionalists frequently be greater than that of the traditional aristocracy, but their power in terms of industry and possibly also of government may be greater. Furthermore, their area of communication is often wider; their social circle international. This is true, for example, of directors and senior managers of the aluminium factory as well as of other industrialists who live in the district but who are otherwise unconnected with Banbury. Initially their power and their range of communications were derived solely from industry. They were not inherited. Looked at from the outside, in terms, for example, of their horizon, some of these people 'ought' to have a higher status than members of the traditional upper class, but so strict are the rules of the traditional class system that although traditional upper-class people may associate with them, in traditional upper-class eyes their status is lower. Nevertheless, outside the traditional upper class their status is higher in the sense that their names are more widely known among lower classes than the names of representatives of the most ancient families in the district. For the non-traditionalists are accorded popular status on the merit basis of their achievements and their contributions to national prestige. With whom they associate outside their business circle depends upon their interests and attitudes, their personality and the manner of life they adopt, and is to that extent unpredictable. Those who send their sons to public schools ensure for them an entry into the traditional system.

Similarly, members of the newer professions are not associates of members of the older professions. They are graduates, but they are of middle- or working-class origin and were educated at grammar schools and provincial universities. There is, in particular, a gap between the doctors and the graduate teachers in State schools, a gap which is resented by some of the latter. In terms of intellectual attainment members of the newer professions rank higher than non-graduate members of the gentry, who certainly do not 'know' them. They have neither the qualification of family nor school to commend them. Furthermore, non-traditionalists of this kind frequently find that their intellectual interests are not shared by members of the traditional middle class in Banbury. The differences of education and occupation, and indeed of goals and aspirations, are great. They are not anxious, therefore, to identify themselves with this class.

In contrast with traditionalists, in the upper and middle classes, the non-traditionalist is, or has been, concerned with increasing his economic status rather than with maintaining family prestige and tradition. He values individual effort above such things, an effort directed to status seen in economic terms. Furthermore, since this is so and since non-traditionalists are involved in change they tend to value established institutions less highly, or they do not value them merely because they are established. For their lives are concerned with the new rather than with maintaining the old. The non-traditionalist is not necessarily disloyal or rebellious: his older loyalties are passive, the circumstances of his life do not call them out.

The division between the traditional and the non-traditional worker is of a different order. The non-traditional worker rejects as such the traditional class system and is in consequence a Labour voter (although this may not be his only or his overt reason); he may even be an active local politician—his traditional counterpart is not. In this he shows a degree of activity in formal associations uncommon to his class and particularly to the traditionalist in it who 'leaves things like that to those who know about them' (i.e. the middle and upper classes).

Here is found the denial of the totality of the traditional class system: the situation in which the worker (lowest class) is Mayor of the town (first citizen). Here political status and social class are separated where the traditional system joins them together; leadership is no longer left in the hands of the middle class of the Borough. Genuine embarrassment was felt by the traditional middle class in the town (and by traditionalists of lower status) when their town was represented by a worker as Mayor: 'I don't know how he'll manage'.

Nevertheless, traditionalists and non-traditionalists are not utterly opposed in their ideas, nor are they unaffected by each other. Non-traditionalists in the middle and upper classes are found in Banbury and district who accept some of the traditional values and feel that 'these people (the traditionalists) have got something'. In that case they may try to 'get into' the traditional class system, that is, they try to become acceptable to a 'set' within it. How far they succeed, and at what level, depends on the extent to which they are prepared and able to adopt the way of life and acquire the manners and attitudes of the 'set'. It is easier in the middle than in the upper class, for in the middle class occupation and wealth 'rightly' spent are relatively more important.

Many fail or do not try to integrate themselves with the traditional system, possibly because the level at which they could get in does not interest them and higher levels are closed to them. An example is the provincial graduate who feels himself 'above' the Banbury middle class and yet has no entrance to the upper class. Nevertheless such non-traditionalists try to give their children the 'chances they didn't have'. (This is, of course, also true of the upwardly mobile within the traditional class system itself.) Those who have enough wealth and power send their children to traditional public schools. Those whose equivalence is rather with the traditional middle class send their children to local private schools followed by the county grammar school. So that even though they themselves may have rejected one of the essentials of the traditional system, social inheritance, they accept it for their children.

Similarly, the non-traditional worker accepts many of the traditional class values. Non-traditionalists, like traditionalists, are ranked in terms of occupation, of respectability, and so on. The non-traditionalist has rejected (as impracticable or immoral, or both) individual upward mobility; he has replaced this value by class loyalty and he is concerned with improving the status of his class as a whole. Or, if he does not go so far as to deny the value of individual upward mobility for his children, and many non-traditionalist workers do not, he at least denies the principle of inheritance when he demands equal opportunity for his children with those of other classes. He uses the resources provided by the welfare State to give his child a chance of being upwardly mobile—in contrast to the upwardly mobile traditionalist worker who sends his child, not to the State elementary school, but to a small fee-paying school where stress is laid upon deportment and (middle-class) manners. In rejecting the rightness of the traditional class system and consequently denying the right of the middle class to lead, the non-traditional worker becomes involved in a certain amount of dualism.

This was particularly noticeable, for example, in the attitude to the few middle-class members of the Labour Party. They were accorded no right to lead, nor did working-class members cry off from office on the grounds of being unhandy with their pens. But the (traditional) 'superiority' of the middle-class members was felt (they were, after all, handier with their pens, sometimes they were usefully wealthier); they were voted to office but regarded when there with some suspicion. They were people who had been brought up to a different way of life, who spoke a different language, had different associates, and might they not really be 'on the other side'? Significantly the suspicion was greatest of one who was a member of the traditional middle class, except that he had walked out of the system by rejecting its value premises and had, for the most part, dropped or been dropped by his old associates. But he and his family were known and it was felt that he really 'belonged' on the 'other side', although he was undoubtedly loyal and useful to the party of his choice. No such suspicion necessarily attached to those who came from lower down in the traditional status scale, unless, as in fact happened in one case, they were shown to have retained enough of their traditional loyalties to affect their loyalty to the Labour Party. Nor did so great a suspicion attach to non-traditionalist middle-class members. In some cases they could claim humbler origins, which helped, and in any case they had not been brought up as part of the traditional network of the town's Conservative leadership, for it happens, not surprisingly, that they were also immigrants.

The traditional class system is under pressure from a changing economic and educational system and from the effects of 'welfare' legislation. It is increasingly difficult to pass high status on to children, both because of increased taxation and high death duties. The gentry in particular feel that they are to be the last generation; that their sons will not be able to maintain the standard of life to which they brought them up and, moreover, will probably not feel it worthwhile to try.

Members of the gentry are still returned unopposed at County Council elections in many parts of the Banbury district, but in the town the right of the middle class to unquestioned and exclusive political leadership is successfully challenged. The number of workers who accept the principle that low economic status must imply all-round low status is decreasing, if the high average age of manual Conservative voters may be taken as an index. People of low, but not the lowest, social status now hold positions of the highest status in local politics. Even in the rural areas (those, it must be admitted, nearest to Banbury) social leadership by the gentry, although still usual, is no longer automatic. 'Do you know, it's an extraordinary thing: the chairman of our Women's Institute is a village woman [i.e. not a lady, not a member of the gentry]', said a traditionalist member of the Institute. The traditional principle that class confers an equivalent status in all spheres of life is apparently being undermined in town and country.

Within the town the local traditional status system, under the leadership of the higher status groups in the middle class, rests upon a stable and a reasonably isolated society in which people expect to spend their lives (even if they were initially immigrants). They see their social goals in terms of this society and see them in relation to every aspect of their lives. Lineage, charitable work, local government service and public works generally, and club and pub associations are important as well as wealth and occupation. For it is a close-knit society in which family, business, and social life are interwoven.

But for an increasing number of people in the middle class Banbury no longer contains their goals. These are set by the hierarchy of industry or the civil service. For such non-traditionalists, social status is not a matter of their total showing in the eyes of the town, but of their individual showing at work and socially in the eyes of their business associates, not all of whom are in Banbury and who for the most part are not involved in the town's close-knit social structure. It is unlikely, therefore, that these non-traditionalists will become fully assimilated into the local traditional system as it has existed in the past.

Nevertheless, in Banbury and district, the traditional system has considerable strength. The advantages of being brought up to your position and of 'knowing where you are' are considerable. Members of the traditional upper and middle classes, despite the changes that are taking place, have a personal sense of security of position that is not felt by non-traditionalists, who have to make their own positions and maintain their status on merit alone. From this follows the desire of the traditionalist to maintain his family position and so to train his children that they will also maintain it. The division into public, private, and State schools, and the status popularly accorded to them in that order, supports such desires. Non-traditionalists who accept these principles and send their children to the school traditionally appropriate to their class are turning their children into traditionalists by the second generation. There are a few middle-class non-traditionalists in Banbury who send their children to State schools throughout their educational careers, but they are as few in number as the middle-class socialists. The traditional principle of inherited class position is thus accepted by the majority of middle-class non-traditionalists. Doubtless the traditional system and its values will continually and subtly change as it has done historically. The pressure of the needs of modern industry and government, increasingly felt in Banbury, ensure that although the principle of social inheritance is accepted, the non-traditional merit basis of judging and selecting leaders cannot be ignored.

It is significant also that those workers who have become leaders in trade unions and local government in Banbury have thereby increased their social status within the working class. Some of them must in fact be placed at least on the frontiers of the middle class although they still call themselves members of the working class. This is in a sense an inversion of the traditional class situation. There, higher class meant higher political status; here higher political status increases social status, although it may not alter social class. It is significant, too, that some of these working-class leaders were men who tried, and failed, in the 1930's to be upwardly mobile in a more traditional sense, although not in Banbury. They had started to work on their own account or as small masters, but on failing came to Banbury to find work. Perhaps it is permissible to look upon their new positions as an alternative route up a newly developed non-traditional status scale.

In sum, it is a time of change in the class patterns of Banbury and one in which it is not possible to construct a class system into which everyone may be fitted, nor one in which any simple index of social class may be suggested. That is to say, no one factor such as occupation makes it possible to predict where an individual precisely falls. That social class exists is undeniable; indeed, it is probably the single most profound division in Banbury and district today. Its importance lies in the still very great differences in the manner of life, attitudes, and beliefs of the three classes: differences so great that any intimacy between members of each is difficult, if not impossible. And it is these differences which are the essence of social class distinctions.

## Suggestions for Further Reading

A. H. BIRCH, *Small Town Politics* (Oxford: Oxford University Press, 1959). Although this study of Glossop is not altogether comparable with Mrs. Stacey's *Tradition and Change,* there are interesting comparisons between them because Glossop is a small industrial town of about the same size as Banbury, located however much further north, near Manchester.

T. BRENNAN, E. W. COONEY, and H. POLLINS, *Social Change in South West Wales* (London: Watts, 1954). In this study the emphasis is on change, particularly as related to the industrial development of South Wales since the beginning of the century. Special attention is given to the effect of these changes on religious and political affiliations, and their relationship with the class system is very well described.

RONALD FRANKENBERG, *Communities in Britain* (Harmondsworth: Penguin Books, 1966). An excellent account of social life in British towns and countryside based upon a summary of a large number of empirical inquiries, including *Tradition and Change,* carried out in Britain since the end of the Second World War. Frankenberg also discusses the theoretical basis of social change in communities.

JOHN MADGE, *The Origins of Scientific Sociology* (London: Tavistock Publications, 1963), ch. 5, "Life in a Small Town." A thoughtful appraisal of the work of the Lynds in America, this chapter may nevertheless be read in conjunction with *Tradition and Change* as an indication of the level of theoretical sophistication which is nowadays required in studies of this nature.

CHARLES VEREKER and J. B. MAYS, *Urban Redevelopment and Social Change* (Liverpool: Liverpool University Press, 1961). This study by the community research section of the Social Science Department at Liverpool University is directed toward the effect on community life of planned changes brought about by the Liverpool City Corporation in the 1950's. It deals with part of the central area of a large conurbation and is accordingly concerned with rather different problems from those facing the inhabitants of Banbury. The social class factor, for example, does not arise, but the study is useful as a further example of the use of many techniques of inquiry by English social scientists.

PETER WILLMOTT, *The Evolution of a Community* (London: Routledge and Kegan Paul, 1963). A study of Dagenham, near London, by comparison with a study of the same town made forty years before, this survey made by the Institute of Community Studies may usefully be compared with *Urban Redevelopment and Social Change* as a further example of the effect of planned development in a conurbation.

# ᴧCoal and Conflict

W . H . S C O T T , E N I D M U M F O R D ,
I . C . M C G I V E R I N G , A N D J . M . K I R K B Y

*One of the most striking features of British society since the out-
break of the Second World War has been the extent to which every
government, irrespective of its political outlook, has sought to imple-
ment national policies which would bring about major changes in
some aspect or other of the social system. Perhaps even more striking, however, has been the persistence of a general belief, especially
in the postwar period, that such policies have been largely negated
by the traditional attitudes of those most subjected to them. Thus
almost every measure of the welfare state has been said at some time
or another to have gone astray, because instead of being met in the
spirit intended, it has been regarded with suspicion or, alternatively,
ruthlessly exploited.*

*An outstanding example of this belief is to be found in the case
of the nationalized coal industry. In the interwar years relations between employers and employees in this industry were very bitter
indeed, and the only instance in British history of a general strike
was provoked in 1926 by this hostility. In 1947, consequently, the
new controllers of the industry, the National Coal Board (N.C.B.)
and its subsidiary organizations, faced a formidable task. The mea-*

SOURCE: W. H. Scott, Enid Mumford, I. C. McGivering, and J. M. Kirkby,
*Coal and Conflict: A Study of Industrial Relations at Collieries*, Chapter 3
(pp. 65–110). Copyright © 1963 by Liverpool University Press. Reprinted by
permission.

*sure of their success is to be seen in the facts that after nationalization, productivity, which previously was lower than in continental pits, has been higher, and strikes, as measured by the number of working days lost, have lessened in comparison with the experience of other British industries. But because there has been no decrease in disputes, unofficial stoppages, slowdowns, and absenteeism since nationalization, it has frequently been asserted that the bitterness of the inter-war years has been perpetuated, particularly on the part of the miners. Superficially at any rate, the tradition of conflict has persisted in spite of a very different property and power structure from what originally gave rise to it.*

*Starting from this position, W. H. Scott and his colleagues set out to discover whether industrial relations in coal mining were in fact as bitter as so often painted. They were aware, of course, that the statistics indicated the industry had more than its share of industrial conflict, but they were also aware from previous studies they had made, above all in the relatively peaceful steel industry,[1] that attitudes and conflicts in a single firm vary considerably from occupational group to occupational group, and they wondered whether a detailed study of industrial relations in mining might provide an alternative explanation from that of the "persistence of a tradition."*

Coal and Conflict *provides a summary of their findings in two collieries in Lancashire, chosen for their very different physical conditions and levels of mechanization. Two main techniques of inquiry were followed, supplemented by observation and focused interviewing. For details of the content and operation of management-union relations with reference to the grievance procedures of the industry, members of the research team regularly attended union and other meetings and kept records of all disputes, reaching undermanager, manager, and group-manager level, over a period of eight months from November, 1957, to June, 1958. These records provided the basis of analysis of what the research team called "organized" con-*

[1] W. H. Scott *et al., Technical Change and Industrial Relations* (Liverpool: Liverpool University Press, 1956); Olive Banks, *The Attitudes of Steelworkers to Technical Change* (Liverpool: Liverpool University Press, 1960).

*flict. For details of "unorganized" conflict, other than absenteeism, which was taken from the pit records, a sample of 1:8 or a multiple of 1:8 was interviewed at random from each occupational group in the two collieries, amounting to 22.5 percent of all employees (575 out of 2,608). The interviews all took place at the collieries, often in the pits themselves close to a man's daily work. The questions ranged from personal information, age, history of employment, father's occupation, etc., to opinions on a wide variety of controversial issues, centering on employment, nationalization, and so forth. The results obtained were tabulated and degrees of significance between variables calculated on the basis of chi-squared tests. Few of these tables were actually reproduced in the book, although footnote references were given to them, but the tables are available on request from the Social Science Department of the University of Liverpool.*

*A major part of the analysis was devoted to an examination of indices of morale and conflict, their significance, and their relationship one to another and to aspects of the situation selected for study. In the selection which follows, only unorganized conflict is considered as this is measured by (1) absenteeism, (2) answers to questions designed to tap a man's attitude to the nationalization of the industry, (3) attitude toward the management of the pit, (4) the extent to which a man would like to change his job. In general this extract is typical of the type of analysis used in a study where statistical tests are only the basis from which an investigation starts and not its conclusion.*

In any industry, some of the most important situational differences will derive from variations in managerial policy and behaviour, which will be reflected in differences in organization, in superior-subordinate relations, in the handling of personnel problems and in many other matters. In mining, there is every reason to assume that managerial variations may be crucial, and in perhaps no other industry are both the effectiveness and welfare of the employee so dependent on the quality of day-to-day management. Once again, the ramifications of this statement will unfold below, but three considerations will serve to illustrate it here. Conditions underground, and particularly on coal faces and where development work is proceeding, greatly increase the importance of the normal 'supply' and 'service' functions of management, and much inefficiency and frustration will result at the point of operations if a high standard is not maintained in their discharge. The considerable distance of many faces from the entry to the mine, the physical difficulties often encountered in maintaining the uninterrupted movement of men and material between these points, and the differentiated and interdependent organisation of tasks on the face itself, all emphasise the importance of 'service' functions. Further, these factors, and the frequent occurrence of unpredictable conditions on the faces, place a high premium, in the interests of both efficiency and safety, on close managerial contact with operations, on speedy and effective communication within the management structure, and on the adaptability and flexibility of both officials and management procedures. Again, the variability of underground conditions, together with the relatively high absenteeism of some faceworkers, accentuates the normal managerial problem of securing a stable and effective deployment of the labour force; and the way in which management tackles this problem clearly would be expected to influence both efficiency and, through its impact on the stability of individuals and work groups, employee satisfaction and morale.

These examples should serve to suggest the crucial importance of the managerial contribution in mining, and some of the consequences which may flow from indifferent managerial performance. This is not, of course, to suggest that managerial differences alone will account for other differences between situations in mining, but rather to assume that this factor is the most important, particularly when other significant variables, such as the scale of the operating unit, the size and composition of its labour force and the level of its technology, are similar. However, other factors may well be important, and two in particular should be noted here. Although studies in some other industries have suggested that physical conditions of work are relatively unimportant, provided that other aspects of the situation are deemed satisfactory by employees and that adequate measures have been taken to mitigate any undue nuisances in the physical environment, it would be rash to assume that this necessarily holds for mining. We have stressed that physical conditions are often extremely difficult in mining, that there are often marked differences between pits and even coal faces, and that physical conditions were generally agreed to be worse in Colliery B than in Colliery A. It may be, therefore, that the generally adverse state of physical conditions in mining, and more especially the fact that these may sometimes be almost dispiriting rather than trying, is related to differences in morale and conflict, particularly as the managerial contribution itself may be less adequate when the problems posed by conditions are formidable. Finally, it should be recalled that traditional values may be influential in producing differences between collieries and pits. Some of these, such as the belief that a high measure of authority and responsibility should vest in the manager himself and not be delegated, may be fairly constant, but others may certainly vary, as the differing histories of our two collieries exemplify.

The overall differences between occupations, irrespective of the distribution of their members between collieries and pits must now be considered. These will first be outlined, and then a brief comment upon them will be made, since, in some cases at least, a fuller interpretation must be postponed until the differences between pits have been examined. As regards four groups, however—under-officials, haulage, maintenance, and 'other surface' workers—the variations between collieries and pits are small, and these groups therefore will be analysed more fully towards the end of this section. In passing now to a description of overall differences, we must point out that it may be necessary to make some reference to particular pits, in order to emphasize those cases in which the results have been influenced unduly by the information obtained from any one of them. The results for the question on changes desired are omitted from this initial overall assessment, since they were *post facto,* being contingent on the morale differences established by reference to the other indices. They will, however, be presented when the particular occupational groups are analysed later.

The major differences between the main occupational categories on our indices of morale are summarised in Table 1 below. In each case a √ indicates that the score of the occupational group was significantly *lower* than that for our sample as a whole, and this is regarded as possibly indicative of higher morale; a X, on the other hand, shows that the score was significantly *higher* than that for the sample as a whole, which suggests the possibility of lower morale. Although, as will be seen below, every item in the Table must not be taken simply at its face value, the overall scores are clearly related to the status hierarchy of occupations. Thus, if we assume for the moment that a √ and a X are roughly equal, and if the 'positive' and 'negative' scores for each occupational category are balanced out, there is a direct relation between the status of an occupation and its overall score with but one exception, the haulage group—and, in this case, there are unusual features which help to explain this unexpected result. Thus, for example, the 'positive' and 'negative' scores of the fillers and rippers cancel out, whereas the packers, etc., have a balance of one 'negative' score. Similarly, the maintenance men have a 'positive' balance, but 'other surface' workers emerge with a 'negative' score.

Some of these results must be examined further, but first we may dispose of those which are straightforward and require little elaboration or qualification. At the descriptive level, the tabulated results for under-officials, fillers, rippers, maintenance and 'other surface' workers may be taken more or less at their face value, in the sense that the results are not unduly influenced by any technical factor, whether this be the inclusion of the information collected for a particular colliery or pit, or a bias introduced, in relation to a particular occupation, by the system of classification used. Thus, in general at the two collieries, under-officials do not differ significantly from our sample of employees as a whole, except in respect of absence and job change. [Of course] . . . their lower average absence

*Table 1. General Indices of Morale—Overall Differences between Main Occupational Categories*

| | ABSENCE | CRITICISM NATIONAL- ISATION | CRITICISM MANAGEMENT | DESIRE TO CHANGE JOB | BALANCE |
|---|---|---|---|---|---|
| Under-officials | √ | | | √ | √ √ |
| Fillers | X | √ | X | √ | o |
| Rippers | X | | | √ | o |
| Packers, Cutters and Conveyor Movers | X | | | | X |
| Haulage | √ | | √ | X | √ |
| Maintenance | — | | | √ | √ |
| Other Surface | — | | | X | X |

X indicates that the members of this occupation were significantly *more* likely to exhibit this characteristic than was our sample of employees as a whole.

√ indicates that they were significantly *less* likely to do so.

— no comparable data.

cannot be taken simply at its face value, but even if this score is discounted, their balance is greater than that of the fillers and rippers. The fillers are characterised by higher absence and by more criticism of management, but these 'negative' scores are counterbalanced by their relative unwillingness to consider a change of job and by the virtual absence of any criticism of nationalisation from them. The rippers are in general characterised by higher absence and by a greater attachment to their jobs. Maintenance men are also attached to their present jobs, but they achieved no 'negative' scores to offset this 'positive' one. On the other hand, 'other surface' workers showed less attachment to their present jobs, and did not achieve a 'positive' score on any item.

As regards packers, etc., and haulage workers, it is necessary to make certain qualifications about the summary information contained in Table 1.

The results for the packers, etc. category would be even more 'negative' but for the inclusion of cutters and conveyor movers. When the packers, the largest single element in the category, are considered separately, it is found that they have the highest absence rate of any group—an average of 5.1 periods of absence during the three months covered—whereas there are no significant differences between the averages for other faceworker groups at either of the two collieries. Moreover, and perhaps more significantly, there would be a 'negative' score under 'job change' for this category if it related to packers alone; no less than 67 per cent of the packers in our sample expressed a wish to change jobs if the opportunity arose. In fact, therefore, although the packers, etc. category alone amongst face groups has a 'negative' score, this is emphatically the case in respect of packers alone, and it is their data which produce the 'negative' result for the category as a whole.

At first glance, the overall results for haulage workers suggest that they may evince morale as high as that of any manual worker group, but important qualifications again are necessary. Their position will be discussed fully below, but two points must be noted here. Their lower absence in relation to other underground groups was mentioned earlier, and the severe limitations of a straight inter-group comparison of absence, for the purpose of assessing relative morale and conflict, were stressed. Otherwise, they are the only category which is less likely than the sample as a whole to criticise management, and, apart from 'other surface' workers, they are alone in being more likely to wish to change their jobs. In both these respects the low age composition of the category—58 per cent are under 31 years of age, and 41 per cent under 21 years—is almost certainly the main explanation.

## The System of Rewards

We must now comment on these overall results, to the limited extent which is permissible at this stage. It was noted above that, with the exception of haulage workers, the results were related to the status hierarchy of occupations; as this hierarchy is descended, so the overall score of an occupational category on our morale indices falls. This finding accords with previous similar work, which has shown, for example, that attitudes to private property, technical change, management and trade unions are related to occupational status. This relationship must itself derive in large measure from the association between the status hierarchy and the system of rewards. In other words, as we ascend the hierarchy, the total rewards accruing to a particular occupation are likely to be considered superior, in the eyes both of its occupants and of others, to the rewards of occupations below it, and it will tend to be regarded as of higher status than them. This, it should be emphasised, is not to suggest that there is always a simple and direct relation between status and rewards, for a superior status, as for example in the case of certain kinds of white-collar employment, may persist when some of its rewards have declined relative to those of other occupations; it is rather to stress that in most cases there is a marked tendency towards an association between status and other rewards.

This would certainly appear to be the case in the present enquiry, in the opinion both of the researchers and of the miners. No attempt was made to assess precisely the relative status of all colliery occupations, but the main outlines are clear and would be agreed by most if not all pitmen, and stretch from officials at the top through fillers, rippers, packers and haulage workers to the main body of 'other surface' workers who man the screens and washeries. The relative rewards of an occupational category are closely related to its position in this status hierarchy. A fuller examination of rewards may be postponed until each category is analysed systematically, but some of the more important elements in the system of rewards may be outlined here. Earnings are associated directly with the status hierarchy just mentioned, and the men's own satisfaction with their pay is similarly related. As the status hierarchy is descended, and with the exception of under-officials and fillers, the amount of dissatisfaction expressed over earnings increases. Actual chances of promotion also vary according to the status of the occupational category; no under-officials have been recruited from amongst 'other surface' workers, but when we ascend to the fillers we find that no less than 30 per cent out of the 77 per cent of the under-officials who had had a previous occupation at one of our two collieries had been fillers, and this proportion rapidly diminishes as we descend the occupational ladder. The men's own perceptions of their chances of promotion also accord with the realities of the situation. A substantial majority of each of the main faceworker groups evaluated their chances as very good or good (the actual proportion varying from 70 per cent to 85 per cent), but only 51 per cent of the haulage workers gave these answers and the proportions dropped to 8 per cent for maintenance men and 10 per cent for 'other surface' workers.

The view is often expressed by people in the industry that the relatively high financial rewards of faceworkers reflect their arduous and difficult working conditions. Whilst it would be idle to deny that conditions are most adverse on some faces, it is equally true that the cold, dust and dampness of some screens on the surface are very unpleasant, and the views of the men show that their assessments of working conditions are not really related inversely to the status hierarchy. Thus, whilst there is some dissatisfaction amongst faceworkers with conditions, this should not be exaggerated, and whilst it is true that haulage and 'other underground' workers consider their conditions to be slightly better than faceworkers do, the 'other surface' workers at the base of the status hierarchy are more dissatisfied with conditions than other groups. Pay, promotion and working conditions are certainly primary elements in the system of rewards in the coal industry, although there are, of course, other elements, and these will be considered later. It will then be seen that some of these other, if lesser, elements, are not so closely related to the status ranking of occupations. Nevertheless, it would certainly appear that rewards are, overall, closely associated in the minds of mine workers with this ranking. This is borne out, not only by the evidence already considered summarily, but also by the answers obtained to our question on whether a change of job was desired. The proportion wishing to change jobs increased as the occupational hierarchy is descended, and the number of times a job was chosen declined as one moves down the ladder; thus the higher ranking occupations, such as under-official, filler and tradesman are chosen much more frequently, and the lower ranking ones, such as packer, haulage worker and 'other surface' worker, much less frequently. In general, therefore, we may conclude that the position of an occupation in the social system of the workplace is an important basic influence on attitudes, behaviour and morale, although situational factors may be expected to produce variations. . . .

The under-officials were more critical of pay, hours and their trade union than were most other groups. They expressed less unqualified approval of hours of work than any category except surface workers, and more criticism of their trade union than any other major group. The distribution of their answers about pay provides the key to their general outlook on their rewards. They did not express more clear-cut dissatisfaction as such in comparison with other groups, but they did evince less unqualified satisfaction, more qualified satisfaction and more dissatisfaction with their pay in relation to the earnings of others. This suggests, and the comments of most of the under-officials support it, that it was not so much the absolute amount of their pay which they criticised, but rather their pay in relation to other factors. A minority did regard their earnings as low, or as inadequate in terms of the pay of faceworkers or, as we shall see below, of their own responsibilities. But more were dissatisfied in relation to their hours of work and, in particular, the implications of the 1957 Under-Officials' National Agreement. Many—although these were deputies and overmen rather than shotfirers—pointed out that their daily hours of work were invariably longer than those of other underground workers, since they had to descend first and were usually last out, and that their overtime work was increased by the week-end shift which they had to put in at least every other week-end. Being staff employees, they did not receive extra pay for these extra hours, and these under-officials clearly felt that their basic salary did not take them into account sufficiently. Whatever their views on pay in relation to weekly hours of work, however, a majority were of one voice in denouncing the terms of the recent National Agreement.

Their objections focused on the provision which established a norm of 72 shifts to be worked in a period of 12 weeks, with a bonus paid for each shift worked in excess of this number, and with a deduction for any shortfall, unless the deficit was certified as due to sickness absence. After local negotiations, rotas were worked out at the two collieries so that under-officials worked, on average, about every other week-end but, as one deputy said, 'Even if we never miss a shift in the week, and work a shift regularly alternate week-ends, we get in only 66 shifts in a 12-week period.' It is, therefore, not difficult to understand the feelings of the majority of under-officials whose views are exemplified by the comment of another deputy. "We are paid little more, and sometimes less, than the highest-paid faceworkers, yet we work longer hours in a week and overtime every other week-end.' The under-officials' criticism of their trade union should also be considered in relation to their views on pay and hours of work, for their criticism was undoubtedly accentuated by their experience of the 1957 National Agreement, although the basic factor underlying their criticism seemed to be the feeling that their national officials tended regularly to go too far to meet the wishes of the Board. On the other hand, despite their views on pay, hours and the trade union, we must recognise both that the under-officials enjoyed compensating rewards and that they were aware of the value of these themselves. Their emphasis on security in answer to the question on the effects of nationalisation was noted above, and their staff, the continuance of pay when sick and superannuation combine to make their position very secure in relation to other employee groups. Indeed, it is almost certainly this security which provides the main attraction of the job and, in the light of what we have said about pay and hours and what will be noted below about responsibilities, maintains recruitment to it at an adequate level. The average age of under-officials is much higher than that of other groups—no less than half of those in our sample were between the ages of 41 and 55. . . . This relatively high age reflects the fact that a 'fireman's ticket' is regarded by many faceworkers as an insurance policy which should be sought towards the middle of one's working life, since it provides great security in comparison with the uncertainty which progressively confronts a faceworker as he grows older.

· · · · ·

## Haulage Workers

Haulage workers, on our morale indices, were less critical of management and had a lower average absence rate than other underground workers, but they showed a much higher inclination to change their jobs.

It was also pointed out above that the high proportion of young employees in this group was probably the most important factor to be taken into account in interpreting these scores, and this can now be confirmed. In our total sample of haulage workers, 41 per cent were under 21 years of age, and 58 per cent were 30 years of age or under; but the proportions varied between pits, and in pit A1 no less than 85 per cent were 30 or under, whilst at the other extreme, in pit B2, only 45 per cent came into this age category. The relative youth of the group is relevant alike to their lower average absence, their attitudes to management and the desire of a high proportion of them to change jobs.

A much higher proportion of the young workers than of most other age groups is to be found both in the low absence category and amongst those who did not indicate any definite attitude to management, and this is to be expected. Younger workers in the mining industry are particularly dependent upon management if they are to become established and, in particular, if they are to gain promotion from their initial lower-paid jobs; in this connection, a good record of attendance may be expected, and, of course, their relatively low pay acts as an additional sanction to limit absence. Moreover, most of them have not been employed in the industry long enough to be influenced by 'industrial heredity'; they have not yet formed those close ties with older workers through which norms such as suspicion of management and regular absence may be transmitted. The widespread desire to change jobs is also a function of the youth of the group. No less than two-thirds (26/39) of those in the group who wished to change jobs were under 25 years of age, and this reflects the fact that young entrants, when they first go underground, are given jobs on the haulage, but most of them expect to move on to the much more remunerative facework within a relatively short period of years.

Similar considerations explain two other respects in which the distribution of the replies of haulage workers differed significantly from those of other groups. A much higher proportion of haulage workers gave no answer (or, in a few cases, said 'no change') to the question on the effects of nationalisation, and similarly over two-thirds of them (68 per cent) said 'don't know' to the question on joint consultation. The majority of the haulage workers, of course, would not have had any experience of the industry before nation-alisation, and again the youths under 21 would have had insufficient work experience to imbibe any established attitudes. Whilst a high proportion of most groups knew little or nothing of the arrange-ments for joint consultation, the proportion of haulage workers (68 per cent) who gave this reply was the highest of all, and the same explanation almost certainly applies, for it is the young workers who know least about, and are least involved in, the formal activities of industrial relations.

The haulage workers' attitudes towards their pay must also be considered, for whilst the distribution of all their replies does not differ much from that of our total sample, there are marked varia-tions between pits, and different considerations undoubtedly apply. Table 2 shows the distribution of attitudes to pay by age, firstly for all haulage workers, and then for the two pits A2 and B1, where most dissatisfaction was expressed by haulage workers.

It will be seen that attitudes to pay are not a simple function of youth; a substantial proportion of both young and old express dis-satisfaction, but the proportion is rather higher for the older workers. Additionally, in the case of pits A2 and B1, the amount of dissatis-faction overall is much greater, and is even more marked for adults. These evaluations, like most similar assessments, represent of course

Table 2. Haulage Workers—Attitudes to Pay by Age

|  | UNDER 21 | 21–30 | 31–65 |
|---|---|---|---|
| (1) All Haulage Workers | | | |
| Satisfied | 18 | 7 | 16 |
| Dissatisfied | 11 | 6 | 13 |
| (2) Pits A2 and B1 only | | | |
| Satisfied | 6 | 1 | 6 |
| Dissatisfied | 7 | 6 | 9 |

not just a simple reaction to the amount of pay as such, but also a weighing of this amount relative to the earnings of other occupations. This shows clearly in the comments of the haulage workers. Upon entering the industry, youths often feel that their initial earnings compare favourably with what they could obtain elsewhere, and indeed a substantial proportion enter mining for financial reasons. When they proceed underground, and with the prospect of higher-paid work in the not-too-distant future, a majority remain satisfied, but as they gain underground experience, a substantial minority becomes dissatisfied. This seems to occur either because they believe that they are doing similar work to adult workers on the haulage, yet there is an appreciable disparity between the pay of juveniles and adults, or because they become increasingly aware of the high earnings of faceworkers yet are unable to transfer to facework themselves as quickly as they had hoped. The latter consideration applies in particular to those in their early twenties who have completed training for facework, but who have not yet been allocated to a regular facework job and are still retained on the haulage. As noted above, dissatisfaction was more marked amongst the older haulage workers and here the knowledge of facework earnings is even more important. Most, although not all, of them had been faceworkers, and had had to quit face jobs because of injury or age. Some of them were satisfied, since they had been retained on underground work instead of being relegated to the lower-paid surface jobs, and this was a likely reaction when they had received a pension or compensation for injury which supplemented their earnings as haulage workers. But others resented the marked drop in earnings which accompanies a transfer from facework to the haulage, and this was often accentuated by a feeling that there was little or no differentiation in pay between what were regarded as 'hard' and 'soft' jobs on the haulage.

But the concentration of dissatisfaction in pits A2 and B1 remains to be explained, and clearly is not attributable simply to the age distribution of their haulage workers. Admittedly, pit A1 had a very high proportion of younger workers (85 per cent aged 30 or under), but B1 had 64 per cent in the same age categories; similarly, although A2 had more older employees (52 per cent aged 31 or over), B2, one of the more satisfied pits, had 55 per cent. The different levels of satisfaction or dissatisfaction cannot be explained, therefore, by reference to the preponderance of particular age groups alone. The key to the difference is provided by the further comment which many of the haulage workers made when asked about their pay. They said that it was overtime alone which made the essential difference in determining whether their earnings were adequate or not, and these comments came from both those who were satisfied and those who were dissatisfied with their pay. Some of the former suggested that it was only overtime earnings which made their pay satisfactory, whilst some of the latter said that their pay was unsatisfactory since their overtime work was severely curtailed. This second group was to be found mainly in pits A2 and B1, where most of the dissatisfaction with earnings was located, and is certainly related to the timing of our interviewing programme. The interviews in these two pits were completed after the interviews in pits A1 and B2, and after the N.C.B. had instituted its economy measures in the Spring of 1958. These measures included the cessation of Saturday working and the restriction of overtime on other days to the essential minimum. As a result the overtime and earnings of daywage men, including haulage workers, fell. It seems clear, therefore, as one would expect with employees whose adult earnings were only between £11 and £12 per week, that the margin between satisfaction and dissatisfaction was narrow, and that the balance could easily be tipped by a reduction of overtime work. Certainly this appears to be the only explanation of the marked difference between pits A2 and B1 on the one hand, and pits A1 and B2 on the other.

The only other marked difference, in respect either of the haulage workers in relation to other groups or of their own distribution between the four pits, concerns their attitudes to management. We noted above that the haulage workers tended to make less general criticism of management, and we attributed this primarily to the high proportion of young workers. The haulage workers in pit A2, however, were more critical, particularly of the under-management, and in this respect were very different from those in the other pits, although in pit B2 there was also some criticism of under-management. At first sight this may appear to be due to the age factor, for these were the two pits which had the highest proportions of older employees amongst their haulage workers; although this may be contributory, however, it is unlikely to be the main factor, for in these two pits there was a measure of criticism of under-management from other groups as well. In view of the generality of this criticism, further discussion of it will be postponed until the final section of this chapter, when all the principal occupational groups will have been considered.

Our more detailed analysis, therefore, confirms what our morale indices suggested, that the haulage workers were not a low-morale group, despite their position at the bottom of the underground occupational hierarchy. At the same time, the foregoing analysis has also shown that the age composition of the group, which is exceptional, provides the main explanation. The group consists predominantly of the very young, who believe that they have good chances of moving on to facework, and of older workers who have had to forsake facework, but who in many cases consider themselves fortunate to be retained on underground work. Our analysis of attitudes to pay suggests, however, in terms of morale, that there may not be a great deal to spare. Whilst at the time of our enquiry the economy measures were very recent, and dissatisfaction with pay did not appear to have influenced more general attitudes to work, the persistence of this dissatisfaction, particularly in association with the other uncertainties which have now entered the situation, might well lead to lower morale.

. . . . .

## Packers, Cutters and Conveyor Movers

On our indices of morale, this group had a more 'negative' score overall than other face groups. In comparison with our sample as a whole, the group was characterised by higher absence, and had no countervailing 'positive' scores on other indices. Although the difference was not statistically significant, this category was also more critical of nationalisation, and on the question on changes desired, placed more emphasis on the desirability of changes in the relations between groups. Moreover, this category showed a more marked desire to change jobs than did the other main face groups, although this was not included in the tabulation of the scores on our indices of morale, since the group did not differ significantly from the sample as a whole in this respect. It was also noted earlier that the data relating to packers were the main reason why the overall scores for the category as a whole were more 'negative' than those of other face groups. Table 3 illustrates this, by breaking down the data on the basis of the three constituent groups in this category.

Thus, not only do the packers score more heavily on every item

*Table 3. Morale Indices—Scores of Packers, Cutters and Conveyor Movers*

| MORALE INDEX | PACKERS | CUTTERS | CONVEYOR MOVERS |
|---|---|---|---|
| Absence—average number of periods | 5.1 | 3.6 | 4.4 |
| Nationalisation—per cent criticising | 43% | 28% | 24% |
| Job change—per cent desiring | 68% | 18% | 35% |

than the other constituent groups, but on average the conveyor movers are ahead of the cutters. The scores for conveyor movers and cutters are similar on criticism of nationalisation, but the conveyor movers are much higher on absence and on desire for a job change. A second consideration which must be recalled in interpreting these scores is that the figures for the packers' group itself are weighted very heavily by the data for one pit only, Pit B2. We shall now examine the cutters and then the conveyor movers and finally the packers, but in connection with each sub-group the special position of Pit B2 must be considered. It should also be borne in mind that our analysis refers primarily to Pits A1 and B2, since most of our sample of this category (49/64) was drawn from these two. The general considerations discussed may apply to the others, but the numbers in our sample from them were too small (because the groups themselves were small) to permit a reliable answer.

The relatively low scores of the cutters on our indices in comparison with those for packers and conveyor movers appear even more impressive when considered in relation to those for other face groups and, in certain respects, to those for our sample as a whole. Their average absence is lower than that of any face group, and is only .4 higher than the haulage workers' average in Pit B2. Their score, in Table 3, on criticism of nationalisation, is lower than that of any other major group except haulage workers, even when compared only with the answers of other groups to Question 37 on the shortcomings of nationalisation. The proportion of cutters (18 per cent) desiring a change of job is low not only in comparison with packers and conveyor movers but also in relation to other face groups and our sample as a whole; of the major faceworker categories, rippers and fillers are the most attached to their present jobs, but about 30 per cent expressed a desire to change, as did 42 per cent of the sample of all employees. On the additional item, the question on changes desired, although the cutters' desire to see changes in the relations between groups was a little less than the conveyor movers' and much less than the packers', it was nevertheless much higher than that for other major face groups and for the sample as a whole.

There are, however, particular reasons for the high score of cutters on this item, as we shall see below. These results for cutters are also impressive in terms of the fact that the overwhelming majority of them work permanently on the backshifts—and average absence tends to be higher for such workers—and when it is considered that their mobility (an excess of which is often deemed a source of dissatisfaction and low morale) is higher than that of other face groups. Twenty-nine per cent of cutters were found to have made, during the period taken, as many as ten or more moves from one face to another, whereas it will be seen that only a small proportion of underground workers made as many moves.

It seems clear, therefore, that, amongst faceworkers, cutters are one of the groups which evince the highest morale and are least in conflict with their situation. Indeed, a further analysis of the replies of the constituent groups in this category, on the question of attitudes to management, revealed that only 6 per cent of the cutters expressed outright criticism or disapproval of management. The only discordant note is struck by the 17 per cent who emphasised the desirability of changes in the relations between groups, an emphasis which was shared by packers and conveyor movers. We shall see below that this emphasis was a feature mainly of Pit B2, and in the case of the cutters alone it came exclusively from those in this pit. The cutters' concern focused on the failure of the day shift, and principally the fillers, to complete their tasks satisfactorily, so that subsequent shifts were thrown behind; thus the cutters might be unable to start their own work at the commencement of their shift and later might be rushed to complete it, overtime work perhaps being necessary in order to do so.

The precise reasons for the relatively high morale of the cutters, despite their nightwork and high mobility within the pits, cannot be inferred conclusively from our data, but the factors which probably are responsible seem fairly clear. The cutter performs a skilled job, which is less exacting physically than other facework, because the operation is of course mechanised, and his task is clearly defined and relatively independent of other operations. Moreover, his financial reward is not only relatively high but also, because he is paid on a 'task work' basis, it is not quite so subject to fluctuations as are the earnings of other higher-paid faceworkers on piecework. Over a six-month period, cutters in Pit B2 averaged £16 11s. 8d. per week excluding overtime, their earnings varying within a range of £14 to £19 but with nine out of 26 weeks in the £16–£17 category; and in answer to our question about amount of pay, no less than 83 per cent of the cutters expressed satisfaction.

Whilst the conveyor movers' scores on nationalisation and on 'changes in relations' were similar to those for cutters, they showed higher average absence and a more marked desire to change jobs. It will be seen, however, that their average absence, at 4.4 periods, is only about the average for all major facework groups, and, moreover, that the 65 per cent of conveyor movers who did not want to change jobs does not differ significantly from the figure for these other groups either. On criticism of nationalisation, whilst their score, like the cutters', was relatively low, it should also be noted that criticism was confined to Colliery B, and once again was mostly in Pit B2. The same is true of their emphasis on the desirability of changes in relations between groups, but it will be seen that in Pit B2 a far higher proportion were concerned about this than is suggested by the number who raised it in answer to the question on changes desired.

Otherwise the conveyor movers do not differ significantly, on our indices, from other face groups (except the sub-group of packers), and there appear to be no substantial differences in the distribution of their answers to other questions. On attitudes to management, for example, only 28 per cent expressed definite criticism, and this figure, whilst rather higher than the corresponding one for our sample as a whole, is less than that for under-officials and fillers. The one particular difference, although not large, relates to opinions about amount of pay. On this question, 38 per cent of the conveyor movers expressed dissatisfaction, which although it is slightly less than the figure for fillers and for our sample as a whole, is rather higher than for all faceworkers. This is perhaps to be expected, for although like cutters they are taskworkers and their earnings are fairly stable, their rates are lower and their average earnings are in fact the lowest of any of the main groups of faceworkers.

We may return now to their emphasis on the desirability of changes in the relations between groups. As noted above, this concern was concentrated in Pit B2, where one-half of the conveyor movers in our sample actually worked; and it was more marked there than the 19 per cent of this sub-group who raised it in answer to the question on changes desired would suggest. A further manual analysis of the questionnaires was undertaken to ascertain whether others in our sample who did not raise the matter on this question nevertheless posed the problem in their answers to other questions. When this had been done, it was found that over 90 per cent of the conveyor movers in Pit B2 had done so, usually in answer to the questions on organisation of work or hours, although the figures for other pits were not affected. Thus in this pit there was a fairly general concern amongst the conveyor movers about the relations between face groups, although the packers, of course, raised the matter much more frequently in answer to the question on changes desired. This may mean that, whilst both sub-groups shared this concern, the packers felt more strongly about it. The comments, both of the conveyor movers and of the packers, focused almost exclusively on two aspects of their relations with other groups; they resented the fact that they had to work permanently on the backshifts, and they felt that this burden was aggravated unnecessarily, and often intolerably, by the failure of the fillers on the day shift to complete their tasks. A number thought that it should have been possible to devise and operate some system of rotating shifts, and some contended that it had been done in Pit B2 some years earlier. A few would have been satisfied if the old procedure, whereby they could go before the end of the shift if their tasks had been completed satisfactorily, had not ben discontinued; others considered that men permanently on afternoons should have a rather shorter shift than daymen, so that they could get a drink before the pubs closed or get home rather earlier. But their feelings about 'permanent backshifts' were aggravated by their sense of grievance against the fillers who, in fact, over a period in Pit B2 had often failed to 'fill off' by the end of the day shift, so that extra work was thrown on to the later shifts. This had resulted from various mechanical and organisational inadequacies, and was facilitated by a dubious agreement between management and fillers in this pit. Its consequence for the backshift workers was clear, however, for it necessitated their completing the day-shift work before they could start their own, so that this had to be hurried and was often itself not completed by the end of the shift. It will also be seen that this led during the period of our enquiry to a dispute between the conveyor movers and the management, which led to the banning of overtime by the former. Their feelings about backshifts and about their relations with the day shift are therefore understandable; and at first glance it is perhaps surprising that they should not have felt so strongly about them as the packers, who work predominantly on the nightshift, and that their morale should appear to be superior to that of the packers.

The packers, as we have seen, achieved much higher 'negative' scores on our indices than the cutters and conveyor movers, and indeed than the other major face groups. To some extent, again, these results for packers are influenced heavily by the data for Pit B2, and this is certainly the case as regards their scores on criticism of nationalisation and on 'changes in relations between groups'. On the other hand, this influence was minor in relation to the overall scores for packers on absence and job change. The latter scores, for both pits A1 and B2, were well in excess of those for other face groups. Therefore, although there were additional factors operating in Pit B2, it seems clear that the packers in general evinced lower morale then other major face groups.

This is borne out by a further analysis of the attitudes to management of the sub-groups in this category. This revealed that 38 per cent of the packers expressed definite disapproval, a proportion which is higher than for all other groups except fillers. At the same time, it is interesting to note that another particular analysis showed that the packers alone gave the most unqualified approval of the trade union, no less than 70 per cent of them giving this answer. This is a higher percentage than that for any other group.

An analysis of the packers' answers to other questions showed that, as with the conveyor movers, their emphasis on 'changes in relations between groups' is the key to their situation. Apart from the items already mentioned, the only other relevant questions on which packers, cutters and conveyor movers showed appreciable differences from other face groups were amount of pay and opinion of a changed payment system. On both these questions the category as a whole showed a rather more favourable distribution of replies, and further analyses revealed that the packers did not differ appreciably from cutters and conveyor movers, apart from Pit B2 again, where there was much more dissatisfaction with pay. Indeed, their measure of approval of a change in the payment system, which would have put all the face groups in one 'pool' for payment, can be seen as consistent with their concern about the relations between groups. As we have seen, 43 per cent of the packers raised this on the question on changes desired and these were all in Pits B2 and A1, where most of the packers in our sample worked. Fifty-four per cent of those in Pit B2 raised it, and 33 per cent of those in Pit A1. Their concern was almost exclusively with the same two points which the conveyor movers made—an organisation of work which committed them permanently to the backshifts, and the failure of the fillers on the day shift to complete their tasks, thus allegedly overburdening the backshift workers. Our further analysis of the comments on these matters of all employees in the packers, cutters and conveyor movers category, made at any point in the interviews, showed that 75 per cent in Pit B2 referred to them, but that in Pit A1 there were no comments additional to those given in answer to the question on changes desired. Thus two problems require elucidation. There is the obvious difference between the two pits and, within each, there is the apparent marked difference in morale between packers and conveyor movers, although, as we saw above, the conveyor movers in Pit B2 were as concerned with relations between groups as the packers, at least in terms of their comments over the interviews as a whole.

The differences between pits are not difficult to interpret. The comments in Pit A1 were concerned exclusively with the undesirability of permanent backshift work as such, and there were far fewer of these anyway than in Pit B2. This was to be expected, for the development of mechanised mining in Pit A1 had led to packing being undertaken on all shifts, and thus to a distribution of packers amongst the three shifts instead of their concentration in the night shift as in Pit B2. Further, the easier physical conditions, better management and mechanised mining in Pit A1 meant that the problem of a backlog of work from the day shift did not arise to anything like the same extent as in Pit B2. Thus in Pit A1, there were far fewer packers on permanent night shift, and the task of those who were was not increased by work left over from previous shifts, at least as a general rule.

But the differences in morale between packers and conveyor movers, at least as measured in terms of absence and desire for job change, were apparent in both pits, and in Pit B2, as we have seen, others factors also differentiate between the two sub-groups despite their common concern about relations between shifts. It is clearly not just a question of shifts, for the conveyor movers worked permanent afternoons, and bore the initial impact of work left from the day shift; and although more of the packers objected to permanent nights than did conveyor movers to permanent afternoon shifts, it must be recalled that the high-morale cutters also work permanent nights. A combination of factors must be taken into account, and in Pit B2 these seem fairly clear. Packing is work which the packers consider as hard as any facework, including filling, particularly under the difficult conditions of Pit B2, yet they are aware that they suffer the double disability of permanent night work and lower pay than fillers and rippers. When to these is added the further burden of a backlog of work from previous shifts, low morale is not surprising. It is this combination of factors which helps to explain their lower morale in comparison with conveyor movers, although it may be that the packers experience a backlog of work as a heavier burden than do the afternoon shift, for two reasons. Firstly, their own task is rather more exacting than the conveyor movers', and on top of this any backlog of work may press more heavily on them because it must be completed during the night shift, if the normal cycle of operations is to commence again promptly at the start of the following day shift. So far as the packers in Pit A1 are concerned, they are subject —or at least many of them are—to the same combination of task, shift and pay as their colleagues in Pit B2, but not of course to the backlog of work from previous shifts. We must assume that this is part of the explanation why, in terms of morale, they stand intermediate between the packers of B2 and the conveyor movers in their own pit.

. . . . .

## Conclusions

The overall statistical associations, for our sample as a whole, between the morale indices and the various specific factors about which information was obtained, support the importance attached to managerial behaviour and to pay in the analysis of particular groups, and permit the discussion of these and other items to be carried further.

Attitudes to pay are associated significantly with both absence and the answers to the question on a change of job. Low absentees are more likely to approve of pay, less likely to be somewhat critical of pay, but more likely to be very critical of pay. Little importance need be attached to the latter, for the numbers involved are very small; one would expect this small group to consist largely of the lower-absence, lower-paid 'other underground' workers, but in fact it is a small number of individuals distributed over the several groups which tended to be more critical of pay. In the case of the question on a change of job, the association is clear-cut and impressive, those who would not change jobs being much more likely to consider pay satisfactory, and those who wish to change jobs being much more critical of pay. The men's evaluation of their pay is also related, although more weakly, to their attitudes to management (10 per cent). A favourable attitude or opinion is more likely to be accompanied by approval of pay, and a less favourable view by criticism of pay.

Apart from questions relating directly to management or to under-officials, none of the other specific factors covered in the enquiry was associated statistically with the morale indices to anything like the extent as were attitudes to pay. Opinions of working conditions were related positively to attitudes to management (1 per cent level), and weakly with a desire to change jobs (10 per cent level), but not with absence or opinions about nationalisation. Answers to the question on security of employment correlated with attitudes to management (5 per cent level), but not with other morale indices. Similarly, opinions about the plant were associated, inversely, only with absence (5 per cent level). However, views about the organisation of work were related significantly to attitudes to management (1 per cent level) and to changes desired (5 per cent level), and these associations will be discussed below. Apart from pay and from questions of managerial and supervisory behaviour, these were the only significant correlations between the data on specific factors and on our indices of morale.

The prominence of attitudes to pay and to managerial questions in the significant correlations for our sample as a whole is, as we have seen, consistent with the frequent recurrence of these factors in the analysis of particular occupational categories earlier in this chapter. Is the significance of attitudes to the organisation of work and to working conditions in our overall correlations—although each showed only one impressive correlation (at the 1 per cent level) with the morale indices—similarly consistent? To some extent at least, the answer is affirmative.

In the analysis of occupations, three particular factors, apart from questions of pay and management, appeared relevant to the interpretation of the morale and problems of more than one occupational category. These three were attitudes towards the organisation of work, towards hours of work and towards working conditions. Organisation of work was relevant in the cases of the packers, the fillers and the rippers; hours in respect of under-officials, maintenance men and 'other surface' workers, and working conditions as regards rippers and 'other surface' workers.

Attitudes towards the organisation of work thus emerge as of some general significance in both the overall and the occupational analyses, and the clear importance of the organisation of work in relation to morale will be seen in the further discussion of attitudes to management and to productive organisation below. The more limited significance of working conditions in both analyses is not, however, necessarily consistent; in the overall tabulations attitudes towards working conditions and towards management showed a positive correlation (1 per cent level), but in the occupational analysis it was the rippers and 'other surface' workers who emerged as critical of working conditions, although these two groups were not more critical of management than were our sample as a whole—indeed, they were less critical than certain other groups. An examination of the overall tabulation of answers to the questions on working conditions against those on management, in terms of the distribution of occupations within it, shows that the category 'critical of working conditions, critical of management' consists predominantly of members of the various face occupations, with Colliery B once again more heavily represented. Thus it appears that the more adverse physical conditions were associated with other aggravating circumstances, such as stoppages and breakdowns deriving from shortcomings in the organisation of work and plant, either the question on working conditions was understandably given a wider interpretation, or adverse physical conditions were associated with critical attitudes to management deriving primarily from other factors.

As regards hours of work, the results of our overall and occupational analyses also appear at first sight to be opposed, but in fact they are not. The three groups which were most critical of hours were the under-officials, and the maintenance and 'other surface' workers; in other words, apart from the under-officials—a relatively small category—no group of underground workers was sufficiently concerned about hours for this factor to emerge as significant in relation to them. It is not surprising therefore that hours of work did not prove significant in our overall tabulations in relation to the morale indices; hours were important to a substantial number only of the three groups mentioned, who thought them excessive in relation to the hours of the main groups of underground workers and to their own rewards.

The associations which emerged on questions of management and supervision are most interesting. The correlations between absence and job change on the one hand, and answers to the question on changes desired on the other, are both very significant (1 and 5 per cent levels). Low absentees and those who do not wish to change their jobs are both more likely to suggest managerial changes, and even more likely to mention the desirability of changes in the organisation of production; whereas the higher absentees and those opting for a job change are much more likely to propose changes in their welfare arrangements or working conditions. Similarly, absence related inversely to attitudes to immediate officials (5 per cent level), the lower absentees being more critical of them. However, the greater concern of the lower absentees and of those who are attached to their present jobs with questions of productive organisation rather than with management or officials as such is suggested by two further associations. Both of these point in the same direction. Whilst those who criticise under-officials or management are both, as one would expect, more likely to suggest managerial changes, those who express favourable attitudes towards under-officials and management are more likely to desire changes in productive organisation (both 1 per cent level).

The attitudes to management and to managerial organisation which have been outlined, clearly do not constitute a simple emotional response to frustration of the kind which it is all too often assumed that employees are prone to make. It is easy to posit that low morale will issue in hostility to management, or that dissatisfaction with rewards or working conditions will be 'projected' on to management or some other scapegoat. Both common experience and previous research suggest that this is part of the truth, but the present findings indicate that it is far from being the whole of it. There is no significant association between absence and attitudes to management, and although there is some relation between criticism of management, and both a desire for a job change and dissatisfaction with pay, both these correlations are weak (10 per cent level). On the other hand, attitudes to management are related very significantly (1 per cent level) only to answers concerning under-officials, the organisation of work and working conditions. Similarly, on the question on changes desired, favourable attitudes to management are associated more frequently with responses suggesting changes in productive organisation than with proposals for changes in welfare or working conditions.

There seems indeed to be no evidence of any widespread hostility to management, but rather a concern with its effectiveness, particularly as this affects the dignity of the employee and the smooth performance of his task. Although the higher absentees, those who wished to change jobs and those who were dissatisfied with various rewards were not characterised by any marked hostility towards or criticism of management, the more positive orientation which has been outlined was most apparent amongst those who, at least on our indices, evinced the highest morale. From the analyses of this group, it seems clear that the predominant element in it consists of established employees who have 'settled', and have become attached to the industry, their pits and their jobs, but who are not so old as to have been influenced to any extent either by pre-war experience or the frustrations and anxieties that can accompany the last quarter of a miner's working life. Their commitment reflects their relative satisfaction with their immediate rewards, so that now they are more 'work-orientated' than their fellows, in the sense that they are more concerned with the general conditions of their work, or at least those aspects which affect directly the performance of their tasks or their treatment as individuals. In the coal industry, as suggested earlier, the effectiveness of managerial organisation and the efficiency of plant are of peculiar importance to the faceworker for the completion of his task, because of natural difficulties and the piecework system . . . . Indeed, the maintenance of certain rewards, including, for example, pay, limited hours of work and the smooth performance of tasks is as dependent, if not more dependent, on productive organisation as on the efforts of individuals. Because of the nature of this link, it is perhaps not surprising that the 'stayer' in a job, in particular, should be concerned about it.

Finally, we may note that at this stage the critical attitudes towards the trade union of a high proportion of this group is perhaps their one characteristic which is most difficult to interpret. The comments suggested, in the main, that the union was too prone to give general support to managerial policies rather than to challenge, when necessary, their particular and local application, and thus a number felt that their specific problems were not accorded adequate attention by their union. The age distribution of the group again suggests that lack of pre-war experience and thus a limited awareness of the union's past struggles and of its contribution to the basic changes in the industry, may be relevant. Most criticism of the union in fact came from the 31–40 age group, and this was also true of our sample as a whole, but this can be only a very partial explanation, for the 21–30 age group was somewhat more approving than others, both in this group and in the total sample. The fact that in this high morale group the 31–40 age category consisted almost entirely of faceworkers and under-officials may be more relevant. . . .

Overall, we may say that low morale appears clearly to be associated with dissatisfaction about pay. Again, as in the case of attitudes to management, this is not to be explained simply as the displacement into a conventional channel of dissatisfaction arising from other sources; the associations between other factors and our indices were weak in comparison with the correlations involving attitudes to pay, and in the occupational analysis it seemed clear that under-officials, surface and haulage workers had pay problems which appeared important in their own right; moreover, whilst the pay of faceworkers is higher than that of other manual grades, the instability of their earnings is an important factor . . . . It is much more difficult, for our sample as a whole, to define the conditions which might be expected to promote the highest morale, given satisfaction with immediate rewards. The particular category of higher morale employees which has been analysed was, of course, an aggregate drawn from all occupations, and the factors in each case may well differ. It would require an enquiry of a different kind from the one undertaken to permit generalisation about the particular factors which may have operated to produce higher morale amongst the members of this category; for example, more intensive study of the specific circumstances of the individuals concerned would be necessary, whereas our enquiry, for the most part, allows tenable conclusions to be drawn only about factors which either differentiate between entire occupational categories or are common to several of them.

The factors deemed relevant to differences in morale between occupations were analysed earlier, and it will be recalled, for example, that in the cases of the cutters and rippers it appeared that their relative independence of the activities of others and thus of close managerial supervision almost certainly contributed to their higher morale. Over the work force as a whole, on the basis of our analysis of the higher morale category, it would appear that a similar factor is operative. When immediate rewards are considered reasonable, and particularly when for this or other reasons an employee becomes a 'stayer' at his colliery and job, effective productive organisation and managerial behaviour would appear to be conditions for the achievement of really high morale.

## Suggestions for Further Reading

R. K. BROWN, "Participation, Conflict and Change in Industry," *The Sociological Review*, XIII (November, 1965), 273–950. A review of the research in industrial sociology carried out in Liverpool which thoroughly discusses its strengths and weaknesses.

————, "Research and Consultancy in Industrial Enterprises," *Sociology*, I (January, 1967), 36–60. A review of the industrial work carried out by the Tavistock Institute of Human Relations which parallels Brown's earlier review of the work at Liverpool.

T. LUPTON, *On the Shop Floor* (London: Pergamon Press, 1963). A study largely based on participant observation in garment manufacture and the manufacture of electrical components; although the general context is different, the importance of the wage structure as an influence on satisfactions and morale emerges equally as strongly as in *Coal and Conflict*.

w. h. scott *et al., Technical Change and Industrial Relations* (Liverpool: Liverpool University Press, 1956). This study by the industrial research section of the Social Science Department at Liverpool University worked out a framework for research into the impact of technical and organizational changes on the occupational structure of an enterprise, in this instance the steel industry. It set the context for the later research reported in *Coal and Conflict*.

e. l. trist *et al., Organisational Choice* (London: Tavistock Publications, 1963). Another major research center in industrial sociology in Great Britain is the Tavistock Institute of Human Relations, which is independent of the universities and undertakes consultancy for firms as well as conducting pure research. This study is of the impact of changing mining technologies on the group structure of coal face workers and hence supplements the more sociological enquiry reported in *Coal and Conflict*.

# Sects and Society

B R Y A N   R .   W I L S O N

*Throughout its history European sociology has always given a central place to the study of conflict in social life, particularly emphasizing those instances where conflict has taken the form of organized protest. It has in consequence given considerable attention to the ideological basis of such protest movements and sought almost invariably to relate them to the value systems of the various status groups in society. Inevitably, the study of other minority groups has been influenced by this perception.* Sects and Society *is no exception to this rule. Bryan Wilson has taken as his subject matter the history, doctrine, organization, social teachings, and social composition of three minority religious groups in contemporary Britain—the Elim Foursquare Gospel Church, the Church of Christ, Scientist, and the Christadelphians—and he has attempted to show how each aspect of the life of these bodies interacts with the others.*

*Of necessity much of the study is descriptive, partly because the beliefs and practices of these sects will be unfamiliar to most readers, and partly because Wilson was working entirely on his own and preferred to conduct the research as a participant observer in one congregation in each church studied. It is true that he asked members for information about the organization and the doctrines, under-*

SOURCE: Bryan R. Wilson, *Sects and Society: A Sociological Study of Three Religious Groups in Britain,* Chapters 4 and 5 (pp. 78–118). Copyright © 1961 by Bryan R. Wilson. Reprinted by permission of Heinemann Educational Books and the University of California Press.

*took interviews to obtain life histories, and read the journals, biographies of leaders, tracts, sermons, and other documents to get a deep appreciation of what membership entailed. He found, however, that winning the confidence of sectarians was a lengthy and delicate business, and this confirmed his conviction that participant observation, rather than structured interviewing for statistical purposes, is an essential technique for the study of social movements.*

*The passage which follows is from the investigation of one sect only, the Elim Foursquare Gospel Church, a revivalist movement that spread to England from America before the First World War. Wilson's chapters on the Christian Scientists and the Christadelphians take a similar form, and although he leaves his sociological analysis to the concluding chapter of the book, it obviously influenced his handling of the descriptive material. The lack of statistical data may, however, be seen as a disadvantage; and indeed there are a number of statements which are quantitative in implication although Wilson's methods prevented him from giving numbers and percentages. His references to "some" or "most" may in that sense be read to indicate that with greater resources more precise results might have been obtained, provided that the suspicions of the sect members could have been overcome. Nevertheless, in spite of these limitations,* Sects and Society *remains an excellent example of what one researcher can achieve entirely on his own, if a clearly understood, sociological frame of reference colors his perspective.*

## The Social Teachings and Practices of Elim

The members of the Elim movement are expected to spend the greater part of their leisure time in the church or assisting with its activities. In the smaller churches in particular almost everyone has opportunity to know everyone else. In addition to the usual church meetings it is quite frequently the case that groups of members will meet together for social and devotional occasions. Visiting each other's homes for prayer and hymn-singing is a common practice among Elimites, and the family spirit prevails within the church community. Bickerings, rivalry and jealousies inevitably occur within the local group in the nature of family tiffs; petty spites are vented, grievances aired, reconciliations effected. Normally the members of the Elim group are relatively unacquainted with doctrinal matters, are not consulted in procedural matters and are impotent to alter church organisation—so that such divisions cannot readily be rationalised and elaborated. Differences can occur at such highly personal levels only in a group which draws its members together into a close community; were the Elim church more a *Gesellschaft* and less a *Gemeinschaft* such differences would no doubt require a more explicit rationalisation, and would tend to occur less frequently. But in the Elim group association is far closer then mere polite relationship; it is a group in which emotionalism is encouraged; and it probably selectively recruits those disposed to such an emotional approach. These factors assist in promoting factious behaviour, but make less necessary intellectual rationalisations of such divisions. Frictions remain personal, and are thus often much more easily resolved.

Although concerts, social evenings and bazaars are strictly outside Elim's range of activity, the movement does encourage its members to come together for social occasions as well as for the religious activity which is its normal routine. In many ways it attempts to make normal social occasions into religious occasions, or induces its followers to obtain their social gratification from religious occasions. The movement has, over the years, established a number of houses at seaside towns and encouraged its members to take their holidays there 'in a Christian atmosphere'. It has promoted camps for young people, not all of whom need be Elim members, although prayer and choruses are a regular feature of the camp activity, and the boast of such occasions has been in terms of the number of youngsters who have, whilst on holiday, been saved. Elim's attitude is that all life should be subordinated to the religious, and particularly to the movement's own evangelism. Naturally Elim churches have no clubs, promote no dances, whist drives, film shows, or any of the other recreational activities encouraged in many denominations. When others are on holiday, the members of the Elim movement are holding their convention services—at a national level at Easter and sometimes at Whitsuntide, and at the level of the district presbytery on other holidays, and weekly on Saturday evenings in many, if not all, churches. Or if there are no convention services on such days Elim members are encouraged to go out among those who are seeking pleasure and bring to their notice the importance of seeking first the Kingdom of God.

### Personal Purity—in Theory and Practice

Generally it may be said Elim has inherited a form of otherworldly asceticism which typified Calvinism and, later, Methodism. Earning-patterns and producing-patterns are not even considered as activity upon which religion should pronounce so long as honesty is observed; the weight of religiously-prescribed restrictions falls on expenditure patterns (in terms of both time and money). Labour is a discipline, accepted since it is an essential: it goes unquestioned. But the use to which income is put, and the expenditure of leisure time, is the sphere in which the evangelical feels himself particularly competent to judge. Leisure and leisure habits are the particular point at which activity is regarded as 'worldly': the activities of labour and money earning are simple economic necessities, and on these no stricture is made. Indeed to some extent work may sanctify certain activities not otherwise to be condoned for their own sake—'time spent playing games, reading and walking is not wasted if we go back to our work benefited in soul and body—but Christians must be guided by God'. Pleasure in particular typifies worldliness, and the engagement in spare-time activity which is not in some sense associated with religion, or with the promotion of the word, tends to incur disapproval. This indifference to the economic sphere reflects the age in which Elim has emerged—an age in which labour tends to become depersonalised and dissociated from all other elements of the individual's life. Labour is a mere contractual necessity, virtually regarded as outside the free-will area of the individual's life. Its sphere of operations is divorced from home, from family, from friends and from religion; it is not one of the individual's own real interests. The individual's life is concerned with his consumption activities rather than with his production activities; through division of labour and specialisation, his production activities have become entirely divorced in content from all his interests.

The pattern of the puritanism of Elim follows a well-defined mosaic. It reflects, more or less faithfully, the puritanism of Methodism of a hundred or more years ago. It seeks to crowd out habits and pastimes which in any way deflect a man from God. It is taken as axiomatic that members are teetotallers and non-smokers. In fact some members of the church do smoke, and this has been acknowledged in the movement's periodic literature. Smoking is a far more likely lapse than is drinking; many of those who come into Elim have experienced the long traditional opposition of the Christian life towards drink; smoking has less usually fallen under stricture. Drinking too, normally involves a special visit to licensed premises, and mixing with people who are themselves worldly, and who might, if aware of the Elimite's faith, upbraid him and mock him for his indulgence, in a way only slightly less disturbing than the censure he would receive from his own church brethren, or, more probably, from the Elim minister. The world itself recognises that the religious often hold drink for an evil, but they are less acquainted with attitudes which condemn tobacco. Smoking is a personal, and drinking a social, habit, and this difference makes aberration from the Elim norm more likely in the former case than in the latter. Many Elimites, however, declare that these habits are ones which they have given up since their conversion, although many were no doubt never seriously addicted to either drink or tobacco.

Gambling and swearing are no less proscribed activities, although occasioning less frequent censure; not perhaps because they are more easily tolerated, but more probably because they are less usual offences in the company of the saints. The Bible is held to be emphatic about oaths, while gambling is seen as fruitless waste of money, often ill-afforded; it expresses too close a concern for the ways of the world, while the Christian's treasure is in heaven. Some

Elimites certainly used to gamble before their adhesion to the movement (or to evangelical Christianity generally), and some even
declare that but for being Christians they would still do so: 'If I
wasn't a Christian I'd have a crack now on the pools: I'd go for
£75,000 everytime.' The Elim Christian has, however, other interests for his time and money. In the matter of swearing, fewer
have been affected by their changed religious belief, although one
woman told the writer that she had joined with her fellow workers
in a factory in their usual language: 'I weren't no better than the
rest; dirty jokes as well.' All this is told, however, in the way of con-
fessing past faults, the more readily acknowledged because they are
a testimony to the regenerative power of Christ.

In the early days of the Elim movement, occasional voices were
heard in condemnation of women's fashions, and warnings about
dress were given, prohibiting the wearing of worldly dresses on the
basis of I Timothy ii 9, but concern about such matters has disappeared. Even when condemned by the magazine, such things are
still matters of opinion. An isolated magazine article has not the
weight of canon law, although the magazine does serve as something of a court of appeal for those who are in a dilemma about their
own standards, or those of others.

. . . . .

## The Rejected Wisdom of the World

The sect in the modern world frequently finds that literal
biblicism brings it into conflict with scientific thought, particularly
regarding the origins of the earth and the development of man, and
this difference of opinion involves them in differences with the
educational system and thereby, ultimately, with the agencies of the
state. Theoretically the sect withdraws from the state, giving a
minimum obedience. But as the state increasingly interprets its rôle
as affirmative and active, proscribing what was once permitted, and
prescribing what was once permissive, so the latent antagonisms of
the sect and the world are brought into higher relief, and the state

becomes the agency of the world and of worldliness. The state's endorsement of the natural sciences has provided the most important arena of open conflict between the sect and the secular society in modern times.

There is a certain permitted variation of opinion concerning Creation among those in the Elim movement, although the extent of disagreement is confined to the alternative interpretations of biblical passages and is not in any sense a doubting of the Word. Most Elimites accept, in so far as the problem concerns them, that there is a gap of unknown duration between the times referred to in Genesis i, 1 and Genesis i, 2.[1] Equally Elim is prepared to permit divergence of opinion concerning the time in which the world and heavens were created, in that the six days of scriptural reference may be symbolically interpreted, but beyond this the Elim theory of creation concedes nothing to evolution. Commenting on the discovery of some skeletons estimated to be 30,000 years old, the *Evangel* declared:

> Even if these discoveries were proved correct it would not disturb believers of the Bible, for it is readily granted that in the unknown gap between the first two verses of Genesis i, intelligent beings somewhat similar to man, may have existed on the earth. We shall wait further information of this recent discovery, and it will not surprise us in the least if this so-called discovery of beings who lived 30,000 years ago turns out to be nothing more than a discovery of beings who lived 3,000 years ago.[2]

Throughout the early thirties in particular the *Evangel* attacked evolution theory in its columns: to the faithful it was a 'fairy tale'. The attitude has remained altogether consistent, and commenting on the news of the discovery of the coelacanth in 1953, the *Evangel* complained:

> The man in the street, who often shows rather a superior attitude when matters of religion are mentioned, gapes in wonder at the amazing

---

[1] *Elim Evangel*, XIV, 1933. Various articles: this viewpoint has also been repeatedly expressed to the present writer by members of the movement.
[2] *Elim Evangel*, XIV, 1933, p. 764.

accuracy of the hypothesis of the scientists. . . . Of course when one is speaking in big figures, a few more noughts help to give importance to geological or marine scraps and confuse the unwary. Hitler believed the axiom that the bigger the lie the more inclined people will be to believe it. Modern scientists appear to work on a similar principle . . .[3]

The burden of Elim's attack on evolution in the thirties was directed at the teaching of the theory in school. 'The sad part about it is that this kind of nonsense is . . . taught from text-books of the tax-supported schools . . . broadcast over the wireless, and headlined across the great dailies and the best magazines. . . . Evolution is the greatest farce ever foisted on an unsuspecting public. . . . More than three out of four of our educators in leading Universities teach this beastly doctrine.'[4] In 1949 the *Evangel* attacked the B.B.C. for its series of broadcasts for children 'How Things Began' and the burden of Elim's attack on the schools is similar: 'Our schools are to be used for the dissemination of knowledge which is both unscientific and anti-Christian.'[5] To Elim secular education is irrelevant, an expression of the wisdom of this world. The only knowledge which Elim regards as of enduring importance is that which relates directly to the Bible, and, in a very subsidiary sense, that which relates to a man's daily labour, the importance of which Elim tacitly concedes. Philosophical and academic studies have no such sanctifying purpose. 'Philosophy is just what Paul called it—vain. Philosophy has given the world nothing. There is such a mistaken idea among preachers that they must make a show of scholarship.'[6] It is better that the minister feel himself inspired and called, rather than educated, for his position. Education often leads a man to embrace the criteria of the world, to embrace dangerous, heretical and intellectual conclusions of higher criticism and modernism. In more recent years a cautious but more liberal attitude has occasionally received expression.

[3] *Ibid.*, XXXIV, 1953, p. 28.
[4] *Ibid.*, XI, 1930, p. 129–31.
[5] *Ibid.*, XXX, 1949, p. 513.
[6] *Ibid.*, XII, 1931, p. 380.

Pentecostal evangelism . . . throws open the door of the work of the ministry to the entirely unlearned and ignorant so long as they manifest undoubted spiritual power and ability. This implies no fanatical disdain for culture and education. A genuine Pentecostal church will have plenty of room for these unique contributions to its thought and ministry which only reverent and consecrated scholarship can supply. The Holy Ghost . . . places no premium upon ignorance. But neither does he place a premium on schools and colleges.[7]

Elim members have usually received only elementary education, although there are a few who hold fairly responsible positions of employment. The attitude towards education is by no means uniform. Some are very much in favour of education for their children, but almost always it is stressed that religious education should come first, and that no one should be educated secularly at the cost of religious development. Others, however, are far less trustful of education, and consider it in itself an evil. An extreme expression of this viewpoint was put forward by one woman:

Education is killing Christianity. I can go back to my young days among the Peculiar People; I had an uncle who couldn't read or write, but he got saved, and after that God taught him to read the Scriptures. But now head knowledge gets into religion. It makes young people query the virgin birth. They forget that God can do impossibilities—if they were ignorant they would take it as read. It is the more difficult for a person the higher the education; Christ sought ignorant fishermen—it started among the ignorant. The less education the more quickly you can accept salvation—unless you become as a little child. You don't need education for spiritual welfare; education must take second place.

The more usual approach is to assert the need for religious before secular instruction, yet there is also a vague recognition of the antagonism between education and religion, and a half-assumption that if the individual receives educational opportunities he may not need salvation; an assumption that his way of life is excusably different from that of those in the sect. There is a recognition that the group is composed of the relatively uneducated, and its mission and

[7] D. Gee, *Why Pentecost?*, 1944, p. 44.

expression is recognised as in some sense incongruous for educated people.

## The Issues for Social Action

Only occasionally have Elimites been led into public activity on social issues—against the cinema by preaching at queues and urging people to seek better things, or in active work against public houses.[8] But the onus of such effort has remained with local preachers and not with the central organisation. In addition there has sometimes been movement support for the efforts of the Evolution Protest Movement,[9] or for the Lord's Day Observance Society. The movement has avoided all political involvements, and political allegiance is left an open question for members. In practice many Elimites find no issue of conscience in political activity, but many are unconcerned, and do not vote. Such withholding is, however, more a consequence of preoccupation with other things, rather than a deliberate refusal to be embroiled in political decisions. The writer found no active political workers among the members of the Elim Church. Membership in outside associations is not specifically forbidden to members of the movement, although such interests are not encouraged, and they would, if taken seriously, tend to militate against the religious interests of members. True Elim Christians cannot be Freemasons.

Up to a point patriotism and loyalty to the state are encouraged, although the Church can be critical of state activity—as in the case when too much deference appears to be accorded to Roman Catholics by the state, or when members of the royal family indulge in racing, or gambling, or fail to observe the Lord's Day. In war years allegiance to the state is strained, and on the issue of military service the Elim Conference of 1935 declared that although the movement was loyal to the king, there was an incompatibility of the Gospel call and

[8] *Elim Evangel*, XXVIII, 1947, p. 152 and XVII, 1936, p. 608, article 'Fighting the Pope and the Pubs'.
[9] *Ibid.*, XXX, 1949, p. 513.

the Christian's participation in war, although this "is a matter which every believer should settle for himself in the light of the Word of God.'[10] Thus Elim took up a position which virtually left the decision to the individual, whilst at the same time expressing the firm opinion of the general council on this issue. Yet the movement regarded its members as having a responsibility to pray for Britain's victory in arms, because Nazi ideology would destroy Christianity: God would protect Britain, since she, together with the United States, Sweden and one or two other countries, protected Protestantism. Here was an ambivalence unusual among sectarians. In peacetime Elim had shown its patriotism by the telegram sent to the King, expressing the loyalty and goodwill of the movement from the annual Easter Convention. A movement which permitted such expression of attachment to earthly kings could hardly demand that its members stand aside from the nation's interest in wartime.

In a sense there were two noticeable strains within the movement: on the one hand the sectarian and separatist tendency which sought an insular interpretation of the movement's aims, and eschewed contact with the world in every sphere; and on the other, the loyalist and popular, seeking recognition and approbation from temporal powers, courting publicity and popular regard. These strains conflicted on such issues as that of national service—although no parties emerged in the crystallisation of these viewpoints. These are, respectively, the typical sectarian and denominational approaches to the problem of accommodation. The matter of military service is perhaps the most spectacular instance of sudden imposition by the state of its will over that of individuals. It is an issue which forces the sect to decide in a concrete situation, whether it will accept or reject the world. Where voluntaristic activities are concerned the sectarian's feud with society remains latent, but where compulsory activity is enjoined, the test of principles, or the basis on which principles are formed, is made apparent, and the individual must decide whether to accept or reject the coercion of the state. The choice becomes obvious to all society, and illustrates how far the sect is in conflict with the

[10] *Ibid.*, XX, 1939, p. 298.

mass of men, and how far it will regard as a burden on itself the life and death struggles of the society in which it is permitted to exist. That Elim should leave the ultimate choice to its members is in itself an indication of the compromise with the real sectarian spirit which the pastors of the movement preferred, but into which attitude they could not carry even the majority of their followers. I have met very few lay Elimites who have been conscientious objectors. The same uncertainty of attitude towards the state is revealed in the very infrequent mention in the movement's literature of the question of whether Christians should vote, on which there is no hard and fast opinion. The movement's attitude to social and political questions is not the emphatic withdrawal of the typical small sect, but it is an uninterested and ignorant disdain of such matters, which becomes a response only when the movement is forced to face them, and even then the issue is left as one of individual conscience. Elim comes to conclusions of the denominational kind, but the very fact of pro and con discussion reveals the strong sectarian tendencies within the movement—tendencies evident in the ministry rather than in the laity, upon whom the sect ethic cannot be rigorously imposed.

Throughout its literature, the Elim movement nowhere emerges as in any way opposed to the existing economic structure of society. It accepts social conditions and the economic basis of those conditions as if they were self-perpetuating, unchanging, unchangeable, and unchallengeable. It has little to say of wealth or poverty, and nothing of man's deserts. It has no advocacy of improvement schemes or social reform. Little is said about wealth, but that little faithfully echoes Wesley. 'Riches,' says the *Evangel*, 'crowd out the Lord. Riches create so many responsibilities and open up so many doors of activity, that the word of God is largely crowded out.' [11] But Elim has not been faced as yet with the problem which Wesley saw in early Methodism—the maintenance of religious fervour among those who were acquiring wealth.

Charity is a virtue of which little is said in Elim, although expressions of kindness receive applause when brought to light. There

[11] *Elim Evangel*, IX, 1928, No. 1, January.

is no injunction to charitable acts, and this is altogether understandable in a movement in which works are at a discount and faith at a premium. But there is one form of charity which is not only effective, but also obligatory, and this is the giving to God's work—the tithing system.

Tithing is one of the works on which the literature of the Elim movement is most insistent.[12] Gospel sermons frequently treat of this subject. It is the one good work which is specially commended and which is held to bring direct reward; it is an essential of living a righteous life in Christ. The tithe is given to the movement, and its purpose is to further God's work—that is, to support men and women who give their time to God. It is not used for church repairs or secular work, for which other offerings are expected. The arguments supporting the practice are several. God is believed to command the faithful to tithe, yet tithing is seen as under grace and not under the law. Jesus is said to have commended it. The testimony of history is said to be in favour of it—all sorts of people having accepted the obligation to give one tenth. There is held to be virtue in paying God what is owed to him. Finally great blessings will follow tithing—for 'God is no man's debtor'. Even if one cannot afford it, one must do it—blessing will follow.[13] So the reasoning involves argument by authority—the word of the Bible; the sanction of traditional usage; argument by majority. It pleads special virtue, to which its own people, as specially blessed, should respond; it offers future reward; and finally it uses the technique of argument by paradox. Tithing is regarded as a more practical form of worship than other forms—one's contribution may be objectively measured; the individual knows when he has worshipped properly and appropriately. 'Pay tithes and be rich', 'Give and it shall be given unto you again', are the typical slogans occasionally printed in the magazine, with suitable texts from I Corinthians and the Gospels, urging members to give more than the obligatory tenth of one's income specified in Malachi. From time to time testimonies are offered by

[12] *Ibid*. Frequent articles appear in many years; often whole series of articles.
[13] *Ibid.*, VII, 1926, p. 21.

those who claim their personal fortunes have improved after commencing to tithe. Tithing pays, brings temporal and spiritual blessing: 'You will make money by it; not only to spend for Christ doing good, but you will have more for your own use. You cannot afford not to do it.' [14] Most Elimites told the writer that they tithed, but believed that some did not. In other respects certainly they demonstrated a liberality and charity which transcended narrow denominational boundaries. Simple goodwill is generally evident among members of the movement, and their charity within the group is particularly marked and encouraged. Such activity, however, appears to arise from the social atmosphere of the Elim meetings, rather than from the direct teachings of the movement.

Fully in keeping with the fundamentalist position, Elim is marked by an official sabbatarianism. In common with most Christians, Elim accepts Sunday as the Lord's Day, and the movement has sought to promulgate its views about Sunday Observance whenever it has appeared that Sunday might become profaned by secular activities. Here again, in some small measure, Elim has been drawn into social activity in defence of its beliefs. Occasionally it has urged its members to write to Members of Parliament against, for example, the opening of Sunday theatres for the troops during the war years. For the believer the *Evangel* uttered a solemn warning, 'If you begin by making it Funday you will end by making it Sinday.' [15] Sunday, it is demanded, must remain exclusively given over to religious activity and quietness.

Elim appears to offer little additional teaching on sexual ethics to that which is general and conventional in British society. Sexual license and aberration would always be strongly disapproved, although little is written in the movement's literature on such matters.[16] Yet the disapproval of cinemas, dancing and theatres is at

[14] *Ibid.*, VI, 1925, p. 192.

[15] *Ibid.*, XIV, 1933, p. 11.

[16] The *Evangel* has very rarely discussed sexual morality, but during the war years, 1939–45, when an attitude of considerable frankness on the subject was displayed by both the public and, perhaps only following this lead, the churches, the Elim publishing house produced a book on the subject, *This is the Will of God*, by Donald Gee, 1940.

least partly, and perhaps principally motivated by the conviction that these pastimes promote and encourage general sexual indulgence and immorality. Premarital chastity, marital fidelity and the permanency of the marriage bond are accepted canons of conduct in Elim. Divorce is frequently cited as an evidence of immorality. The conventional ethic, conventionally observed, is Elim's position on sexual subjects.

No special regard is given to celibacy within the movement, and scriptural passages favourable to celibacy are ignored. Women are in no position of subservience, and Paul's injunction that they be silent in the churches is disregarded, or, like foot-washing, is explained as a concession to the times and circumstances of biblical and apostolic days, and no longer applicable. Women are, however, not often permitted to minister in Elim.[17] and the elders and deacons in the churches are always men. There is no tendency in the movement to encourage celibacy or discourage marriage. The restriction of marriage for probationer ministers, and the permission to marry required by all ministers from headquarters, appears to be a matter of expediency rather than of doctrinal precept.

Although no prohibition is placed in the way of the marriage of a member of the Elim movement, the church teaches emphatically that it is wrong for a regenerated person to marry an unbeliever. The Old Testament and the New are both declared to be unequivocally opposed to such a practice. In particular II Corinthians, vi, 14 is cited: 'Be not unequally yoked with unbelievers'. By unbeliever is not meant a non-member of the Elim church, but rather a non-Christian. Whilst a marriage within the denomination might be preferred, the Elim movement seeks only to ensure that marriage is with another fundamentalist, for marriage with a modernist or Catholic would be out of the question. The member of the church is persuaded, as far as is possible, to view his marriage from a Christian standpoint, although no sanctioning authority judges such matters in the case of the layman, save that the minister himself might from time to time offer advice. The maxim is, 'Before you

---

[17] To this general rule there have been rare exceptions, although these are not now encouraged. Occasionally a church is in the charge of a woman minister.

marry "Can two walk together unless they be agreed?" ' [18] Elim thus seeks to retain the Christian's allegiance and to protect it from the possibly deleterious influence of marriage with an unbeliever or a Christian who does not accept the verbal inspiration of the Bible. This would, so it is seen, be a sin in itself. It would appear that in the early days there was a great deal of inter-marriage.

Understandably Elim stresses the need to bring children up in the faith. It urges parents to send children to Sunday School, and to give a concrete example to children by leading the life of the faith. The religious life, activity in the movement, is seen as the answer to problems of juvenile delinquency. In particular the 'family altar' is considered a desirable adjunct to the Christian life. As in all its approaches to morals, Elim tends to regard 'being good' as by no means enough. 'The theme of the new era . . . must not simply be "moral renewal", but a return to the message of the old-time Gospel; back to the lasting Christian example born of true faith in Christ.' [19]

. . . . .

## The Social Composition of the Elim Movement

The members of the Elim movement number several thousand people scattered over Great Britain in 250 churches which vary widely in size, and which serve communities ranging from great cities to villages. The Elim Church is not typically a neighbourhood church, even in centres like Birmingham where the movement has been able to establish a number of churches in different districts. It is usually a central church serving adherents who are scattered over a relatively wide area rather than clustered around it. It resembles in some ways the Methodist Church of earlier times, drawing together into a community apart those who claim a special blessing or assurance. It draws out its members from the midst of the wider society into a separate body which enshrines its own ideals and values, and where the criteria of prestige and worthiness are, at

[18] *Elim Evangel*, XXI, 1940, p. 257.
[19] *Ibid.*, XXXIV, 1953, p. 251.

least in some measure, different from those employed by 'the world'.

Unfortunately, for our purpose, the Elim movement is not sufficiently distinctive from either of the other Pentecostal bodies, or even from other evangelical movements in general, to allow for a very rigorous survey of its locations as a means of discovering whether this form of religious expression is typically urban or rural. Some towns may be without an Elim Church because a meeting of the Assemblies of God, or the Apostolic Church is already established; or an Elim Church may be set up in a town only after the way has been cleared by the departure or failure of another Pentecostal group. On the other hand Elim churches sometimes exist in very small towns where it might be supposed that there were altogether too few people to provide a congregation for a minority religion. Yet, although Elim is a separate movement, its appeal overlaps other groups: it is not specifically heterodox in its teachings, apart from its Pentecostalism and its fundamentalism, both of which are shared by some other Christians. Elim offers a more intense religious experience than is usually available or approved in more orthodox churches; it offers a fuller, friendlier church life, and traditional evangelical faith. Elim's appeal relies to a considerable extent on presentation of the faith which has served to comfort and reassure the individual when he was a small child, and when the literal presentation of Christianity was the only possible way of making religion comprehensible. Thus from the point of view of its teaching Elim cannot be altogether classified as separate and sectarian.

## The Rural and Urban Contexts of Pentecostalism

Elim's beginnings in England were partly rural, and it was not without some trepidation that the leaders set out to begin their work in Clapham. The progress made in Essex was largely due to the efforts of George Kingston, who was responsible for bringing George Jeffreys to England; there are, today, seventeen Elim churches in Essex. The revival campaign methods of Jeffreys, with poster publicity and mass meetings, lent themselves best to large urban centres and it was to these centres that Jeffreys took his campaigns. Elim has made many of its converts by campaigns, and thus to discover the character of the Elim movement and its distribution, one must recognise the factor of conscious direction in allocation of campaigns.

The Pentecostal faith itself, however, may quite as easily arise in rural as in urban settings, and more particularly in periods of social change, when older and more traditional behaviour patterns have subsided or been disrupted. In the United States, Pentecostal movements have experienced phenomenal growth in the Southern States, in areas typified by cultural conflict and social disorganisation, areas of disintegrating cultural tradition.[20] Elim is in no way as extreme as some of the Holiness cults of Tennessee and North Carolina, but it is a religion which emphasises intensely the old religious values. Fundamentalist Christianity is to be found all over the country, and many of Elim's adherents might well, in its absence, join some other fundamentalist church, even at the cost of the specific teaching of Pentecostalism. Many appear to have been recruited from these churches by Elim, and many appear to be only lightly attached to one denomination more than to another.

About a quarter of the Elim churches in England are in small towns or rural areas, numbering about fifty altogether. In Northern Ireland practically all the churches outside Belfast are in small towns. It is not surprising to find the Foursquare Gospel flourishing in such centres. Fundamentalist creeds appear to develop best in groups to which relatively sophisticated public opinion does not penetrate. The absence of any developed critical sense, the acceptance of authority, and a background tradition of faith in the Bible, are often to be found in country areas, and these are ready-made conditions in which Pentecostalism can flourish. When, to these factors, there is added an awareness of the decay of these standards elsewhere, more intense religious expression and fierce reassertion of values may be expected. In market towns and country places there is often a cul-

[20] J. R. Holt, 'Holiness Religion', *American Sociological Review*, V, 1940, pp. 740–747.

turally deprived population, which, once aware of its own cultural retardment, is prepared to capitalise its difference from city dwellers by exalting necessity into virtue, and by giving religious value to the limitations which circumstances alone impose. In the cities such groups exist in a more diffused way, and there are often far more diverse possibilities of outlet for them—there may even be something of an integrated cultural pattern which tends to disguise, or make less relevant, social inequalities, but some appear to be accommodated in fundamentalist and sectarian movements. In Northern Ireland the antagonisms on political and religious issues have undoubtedly assisted extreme forms of religious expression.

The towns in which Elim churches exist are extraordinarily diverse in character, as well as in size. They include such contrasts as Wigan and Worthing, Sunderland and Southport, Bermondsey and Bournemouth, the last mentioned having two Elim churches. It is, however, altogether likely that the social groups to which Pentecostalism gives opportunity for expression exist in most communities of any size, in towns with an exceptionally large proportion of the upper and middle classes, as well as those in which labourers and workers in heavy industries account for a proportion of the population higher than the national average. The socio-economic class from which Elim recruits is so widespread, and so many similar movements are in the field, that no correlation of distribution of Elim churches and social classes can be shown. Various non-quantitative factors also enter into the situation; for instance, in areas where the upper and middle class are more than usually represented, the lower classes, or larger numbers of them, might find greater need for some distinctive religious expression. This hypothesis might account for the existence of two Elim churches at Bournemouth, and for the churches at Hove, Worthing and Southport—all centres where the social influence of the middle and upper classes is predominant, and where, in consequence, the lower class might more intensively require special religious accommodation.

Although no extensive survey can yield accurate information, it is interesting to note the areas in which Elim has flourished. Apart from London and Birmingham, which, by virtue of size alone might stand in a special category, the movement has more than one church in only a small number of places. In Belfast there are eight, but Belfast, with its fierce clash of Protestant and Catholic sympathies, represents perhaps a very different set of circumstances from those of most of England. In Belfast an ardent anti-Catholic tradition provides a favourable atmosphere for a body as aggressive and evangelical as Elim. There is a mixture of cultures, a clash of national loyalties and a tradition of more extreme expression on religious, national and political matters, and there is some social disintegration consequent upon these various issues of intense conflict. Elim is a militant and an anti-Catholic faith of a type no longer so readily found among the more orthodox Protestant denominations, and it helps to canalise emotions into religious fervour, which might otherwise find less socially approved forms of expression. Of other centres, none has more than two Elim churches; two exist at Bournemouth, Hull, Rotherham, Hereford and Bowers Gifford in Essex. The duplication of churches at the last two centres is, in all probability, to be explained in terms of local evangelism. The enthusiasm of one or two people in an evangelical sect is often sufficient to evangelise new areas and promote new missions.

Hull and Rotherham are both towns in which Elim, or some form of Pentecostalism, might well be expected to flourish. Both have large proportions of population engaged in manual occupations, and both are influenced by such factors as shift work, or the irregular incidence of work (sea voyages, etc., dock work, fishing in the case of Hull). Hull was one of the first cities in which Jeffreys campaigned after he established his organisation in England, and there he met with immediate success. Intense religious experience is one way of adding depth to lives otherwise shallow, insecure and difficult. In Hull, with its many families of women and children temporarily bereft of husbands and fathers, religious experience at a personal level, and active communal and friendly church life, at the social level, may fulfil very definite needs. Elim provides both, and Elim achieved great success, not only at Hull, but also at Grimsby,

Cardiff and Yarmouth. But if at Hull, why not at Newcastle, and if at Rotherham, why not at Rochdale and Walsall? To which question answer can only be made that Elim has not, at least in recent years, staged campaigns in these towns, and it is by revival campaigns that Elim's success has been gained and its churches established.

A great deal of Elim's early campaign activity was concentrated in various parts of London, and here a large number of churches were established. Today there are twenty-one in London itself and eight others in outlying areas, and this in spite of the war, when a number of Elim churches in London were destroyed by enemy action, and in spite of the schism of 1940, when the Kensington Temple was lost and the church at Barking affected. The size of Elim's churches in London varies considerably, as indeed it does throughout the country. Of the twenty-one churches in London itself, only thirteen have ministers of their own; two churches share one minister, three have honorary pastors, and three have church leaders.[21] It can be accepted that in the normal way churches which have this type of arrangement are usually the smaller assemblies. The Elim cause has also flourished markedly in Birmingham, where there are fourteen churches, thirteen of which meet in buildings designated as Elim churches, and only one of which is obliged to meet in a hired hall. Three of the Birmingham churches are in the charge of honorary pastors, and two of church leaders.

The Elim churches in smaller towns and rural areas appear, in the main, to be of the smaller type of mission. Of fifty or so churches which are in small towns and country districts in England only twenty have fully-trained ministers of their own; seven share ministers with other Elim churches; two are in the charge of probationary ministers; seven are in the care of honorary pastors, and twelve have church leaders. In some larger centres of population Elim churches are in the care of persons who are not fully-trained ministers. Some of these centres are those in which campaigns did not achieve great success, and where the subsequent churches are prob-

[21] Data relates to 1954.

ably small—such is the case at St. Helens and Leicester; or are towns where the fall-off of those converted has been exceptionally high.

Elim cannot be claimed as an expressly or distinctively urban form of religious expression, although it is a movement which has attained its greatest success in urban areas. In Northern Ireland Elim acted like other evangelistic organisations, of which the Faith Mission is an example, preaching conversion and salvation in the traditional evangelical way. It built or bought mission halls, but its growth was more extensive than intensive. It is significant that in these early days the centres which Elim established were usually designated as 'halls'. In Northern Ireland, outside of Belfast there are listed seventeen 'halls', four 'tabernacles' and only one 'church' in the Elim denomination. This was altogether in the evangelical tradition. Once the campaign had been held and the mission founded, new growth came almost solely from a new campaign. There were inevitably exceptions, but by and large, in any one area one Elim church was sufficient accommodation for new converts who came along subsequently. New branches were added to the movement, usually, only as a result of new revival campaigns, which were generally held in areas to which attention had not been previously given. The new churches were thus generally called into being from headquarters, which has normally sought to make a beginning where the field has not been too crowded with other evangelical movements.

### The Preponderance of Women

No figures are available for the ratio of the two sexes among Elim members. This is not the type of statistic in which the church itself is interested, nor which it would reveal even if the information were available. Nor are Elim churches concentrated in areas with distinctive and unusual sex ratios, so that this line of inference is also closed. Fortunately the Elim movement has, unwittingly, provided some information on this point, in the photographs it has reproduced in its periodicals and other literature. In every instance women form a clear majority of those photographed at campaign meetings; sometimes they are three-quarters of the audience, and never much less than two-thirds. Since revival campaigns have been easily the chief means of evangelism for Elim, it is clear that more women than men have been exposed to Elim propaganda. Observation of several meetings at recent campaigns confirms this distribution of the sexes.

Photographs of special events or services again confirm observation; women are invariably a majority, often in the raito of two or three to every one man. Photographs of groups claiming miraculous healing are a less reliable guide to the proportions of the sexes in the movement. Faith healing appears to inspire more trust on the part of women than of men; or it may be that it seems more effective with women than with men, since in women psychosomatic and nervous disorders tend to be more pronounced, and these complaints are more susceptible to faith treatment than other ailments. Even in the collected testimonies of healing, which are no doubt selected as most impressive, and may be given some artificial balance as between the two sexes, twice as many claims were from women as from men, and this entirely confirms the results reported of other denominations claiming divine healing.

There is little in the formal organisation of the Elim church which offers much opportunity for the services of women, and there can be little appeal to women on that account. Deacons and elders are necessarily men by biblical prescription, and so it is also the case that church officers are usually men. The vast majority, if not all, of the lay representatives to Conference, being usually elders or deacons, are also men. In the very early days when Elim was little more than an evangelistic band, women were accepted along with men as evangelists. As organisation developed, however, the need to pay attention to biblical pronouncements made itself felt, as a defence against criticism, and as support for the claim of the scriptural nature of the movement. A few women still serve in ministerial capacities, a few even as regular ministers. In 1954 there were no women among probationary ministers, and only two in the list of local preachers. In the mission field women do predominate in Elim, being thirty-four of fifty-three missionaries, but few of the women drawn into the movement can be inspired by this very restricted possibility of service. At local level the only opportunity for women is in Sunday school teaching.

Elim does not emphasise feminism, does not stress female spirituality, nor accord to women any distinctively superior rôle in society. Feminism would hardly appeal to the class of people drawn into the movement. The attraction of women into Elim rests on other grounds. Although there is little in the formal organisation of Elim to cater particularly for women, nonetheless the Pentecostal fellowship necessarily provides possibilities for self-expression (directed into certain approved channels) for any or all of its following. And it is here that women so often take a prominent part in Elim ritual. This is an intensely emotional part of the Elim meeting, where each and all may give vent simultaneously to pent-up feeling—in tears, heavy-breathing, groans, utterances of joy and rapture, and, of course, tongues. In all these activities women participate more fervently than do men. There are of course, usually more women present than there are men, and yet the manifest degree of involvement in the spontaneous and ecstatic utterance in Elim services is significantly disproportionate to the sex ratio of the congregation. Women are more expressive at the emotional level than are men. In twenty-five instances of tongues being spoken in one assembly, twenty-four of the speakers were women. It is impossible to state with accuracy how many different women were involved in these exercises over the period of several months, but certainly there were no less than a dozen. In this observation women, too, have proved more frequent vessels of other ecstatic utterances, groans, heavy-breathing and calling out upon the name of the Lord.

On the other hand, these occasions of prayer do provide specific activity for the male members of the congregation, even if these rôles are less spectacular, in the employment of more usual forms of praise. Men more often offer spontaneous prayer than do women but this is a partly institutionalised practice, since the elders and the deacons are expected to lead in prayer, and 'at the throne of Grace' and repeatedly it is these men who break in on the voices of those praising and worshipping for themselves, to offer a more public form of prayer. These are the few men who are most prominent in the church's affairs, and it is altogether their own expectation, as everyone else's, that they should show their initiative in the spiritual, as in the secular, aspects of the assembly's life. Women do frequently add spontaneous prayer of this type, and even at times lead, of their own volition, or after being called by the pastor to 'lead us in prayer'. If for any reason many are anxious to pray, and the prayers are, at the request of the pastor, kept short, then it is usual to find very many women offering public prayer. When prayer is kept short it is less difficult and women who, whilst able to pray profusely in unknown tongues, are scarcely coherent or articulate in their own language can on such occasions very often accomplish the performance with a few stereotyped sentences.

The similarity of this predominance of women with Christian Science and Spiritualism cannot but be remarked. In all three movements women are predominant among the healed; in all three they are the most frequently 'gifted', and in all three they provide the great core of solid support. In Elim, the institutional arrangements of the community necessarily mean that they are more passive than women in the other two movements; they do not become the healers as in Christian Science, nor the objects of awe as do the women who display the charismata in Spiritualism. A principal difference which may affect the different forms of the activity of women in Christian Science and women in Pentecostalism is that of the social class from which the personnel of the two movements are drawn. The atmosphere of the Pentecostal meeting is exciting, individual expression is encouraged, within the established mould, and the individual can win approval, even prestige, and can strengthen her ties with the group, in pouring forth her feelings in the prescribed fashion. For women whose lives are often uninteresting; whose hopes and aims are circumscribed by the home and the factory routine; who have, through the operation of social, economic or psychological retarding circumstances, been restricted in the discovery or employment of more usual social outlets, pentecostal activity might—given perhaps other factors predisposing towards the religious integration of values—provide an outlet and fill a void in an otherwise discontented life.

It is possible that the psychologist could suggest other causes for the predominance of women among Elim adherents. Elim is a cult which centres upon the person of Jesus Christ; it is emphatically a son-religion. During the periods of emotional freedom in the Elim meeting, it is the name of Jesus which is repeatedly uttered, and women are normally prominent in this. At one time Pentecostalism suffered from excesses in this regard—the desire to be baptised into the name of Jesus only, and a development of ecstatic utterance which was no more than the constant repetition of the word, 'Blood'. Today the word 'Jesus' tends to be repeated continually by worshippers. The cult of Jesus in Elim, and the intense emotional experiences which surround the name and the envisaged personage, may not be without profound significance among women who lives otherwise lack emotional expression.

Although it is possible to offer a number of explanations for the heavy preponderance of women among Elimites, it is perhaps also important to remember that women appear to form a majority in most Christian churches, sometimes by proportions not much less than those prevailing in the Elim church. That this should be so does not in itself invalidate the various suggestions put forward to account for female predominance in Elim. Rather it invites the application of these hypotheses to other cases, although it will be accepted that certain of the factors invoked in the case of Elim apply with less force elsewhere. Again, certain arguments put forward concerning the women in Elim have involved consideration of the social class of those within the movement—a factor which cannot always be separated from other elements in the analysis.

### The Social Roots of Pentecostalism

Pentecostalism is predominantly the religion of working-class and poor people. Its beginnings in Britain, although drawing to gether men from many denominations, were predominantly among people who were nonconformist. Fundamentalism was an almost necessary precondition for pentecostalism; its appeal was to those who were already convinced of the verbal inspiration of the Bible, and among the laity such groups are principally to be found among the lower social strata. In Britain it began with the conversion of men in such organisations as the Faith Mission, independent Holiness missions, and even Congregational churches, and among the Plymouth Brethren. The leaders of Pentecostalism were drawn from working-class homes. Stephen Jeffreys left school at fourteen and was a miner before he became an evangelist, and George worked in a co-operative store. Smith Wigglesworth was a plumber. With few exceptions the leaders were all men of limited education and of working-class background.

There is, too, within Pentecostalism, although more implicitly than explicitly, a recognition of the social class to whom appeal is made. The pattern of the movement's activities follows clearly in the lines of the folk-ways of the lower social strata: annual teas; outings by bus to other churches; Sunday school 'treats'; free and easy expression in meetings, with distrust of ceremony and solemnity; the use of 'Brother' as a form of address, with a familiarity possible only to those of known and unpretentious social status. Brumbach, writing primarily of American Pentecostalists, might well have been referring to Elim in Great Britain, when he declared, 'Pentecostal preachers need no exhortation to go back [to "the low, the least, the lost and the last"] for we are content with "our calling"—that is of the common people.' 'On the whole the Pentecostal Movement of today is composed of the same class of people as those found in the church of the first century.' There are few who have attained much in the world who are drawn to Pentecostalism; it is a religious expression of whose who might be termed 'disinherited'. The few occasions when distinguished persons have been present at Elim meetings have invariably received particular and special mention in the movement's periodical literature, to an extent which not only put on display the importance of the person concerned, but no less revealed the unusual nature of such patronage or interest from persons of that class.

The areas of London in which Elim churches are located give some very general indication of the classes who provide the recruits and support for the movement. The Elim churches in London are largely suburban and district churches. The area in which Elim churches stand are predominantly the poorest parts of London, although not exclusively so. Thus there are churches at Barking, Bermondsey, East Ham, Canning Town, Islington and Woolwich; at Clapham, which is the headquarters church, and which stands in an area which has deteriorated, Brixton Hill, Camberwell, Bayswater, Leyton and Ilford. Of the churches supporting a full minister the only surprises are the churches at Hendon and Wimbledon. All the others (five) are in the charge of church leaders or honorary pastors, while two others share a minister. That in general these last mentioned should be the churches in better neighbourhoods tends to confirm the hypothesis that Elim has a predominantly lower-class following. The churches at Ealing and Twickenham share a minister; the church at Sydenham has a church leader, as have the Brixton and Finchley churches, though in the former case there is a church with a minister at Brixton Hill. Hornsey and Wood Green both have honorary pastors. It would appear that generally Elim's success is related to the social class of the district. This broad coincidence does not inform us of the people actually in membership, but it appears altogether probable from what has gone before, that Elim's converts, even when its churches are established in apparently unlikely centres, are drawn from the lower social classes in those districts.

In a local church with about sixty members there was no one who could be described as of the professional class or of independent means. Principally they were factory workers and labourers, with few office workers among them. Generally they lived in small terrace houses or in council houses. Doctors, dentists, civil servants, teachers, lawyers and business men are not found in Elim assemblies. Elim people are usually socially 'insignificant', and often poor. They are members of the working class with very limited material prospects. They are prepared usually to recognise themselves as the 'low and the least', and rejoice in the many biblical promises made to this class of people. In 1948 an unusually explicit acknowledgement of poverty among Elim members was forthcoming in the form of an appeal for clothes, non-perishable foodstuffs and cash for the needy Pentecostal brethren.

Conversation with members of the Elim church illustrates the extent to which Elim eschatology and adventism provide compensation for the deprivation of social, economic and cultural opportunity in life. The dreams of the after-life or of the millennial era are entertained as fantasies or as reveries of the type which wider numbers of men associate with good fortune in this dispensation. Such visions appear to differ little in content from those which follow the pretence of 'If I'd plenty o'money' on which, in conversation, the writer has heard a number of Pentecostalists dilate. There is almost an assumption that those with plenty of money do not need religious experience, and are even justified in living lives of relative ease and contentment, although this would not be openly admitted. There appears to be no resentment of the distribution of wealth in society; the Elimite's assessment of his own position is an analysis of a very different sort, and his desire for blessings is transferred from this scene of operations; his lack of the world's goods allows him to despise the world and its goods. The authority of the wider society is normally accepted; the interest which anyone with any claim to distinction in the outside world might take in Elim is received with pleasure, incredulity and the tacit acceptance of their own way of life as in some sense sub-standard.

Of the education of members of the Elim church all that can be said is in general confirmation of their social class position. The vast majority of Elim members are people who have received no more than elementary education. This is true not only of the laity but of the ministry of the movement. Hardly any of those who have ministered in the Elim movement have had a university education, or anything approaching it. The faculty of the Elim Bible College, as listed in 1926, did not mention any member possessed of a university degree,[22] although many of the subjects to be taught were university subjects. '. . . Church history, English and original languages, Music . . .' At a later date, John Leech, M.A., LL.B., K.C., joined the faculty, but otherwise the various Deans of the Bible College have boasted no university degrees.

Strictly a movement which nominally relies on Holy Ghost inspiration to call forth and guide its ministers, can eschew training in the wisdom of the world, and, on this ground, the absence of university trained men is counted no reproach to the Bible College or its instruction. In counselling lay preachers the leaders of the movement declare, 'We do not recommend reading a large number of books . . . you should read to remember.'[23] This whole emphasis, however, reflects the social origins of those in the Elim ministry, and their distrust of formal education. In fact, Elim is not always disdainful of academic attainment provided that the possessor of such attainment is friendly to the movement. An Elim minister who was successful in gaining a B.D. degree not many years ago was well applauded by the *Evangel*—probably because this was the only degree held in the ministry of the movement at the time.

A movement which evidences so little education in its ministry as Elim will hardly be expected to have a very well educated laity. The very existence of a ministry in so avowedly a fundamentalist group as are modern Pentecostalists is itself an indication of the relative paucity of education among the movement's following. Many fundamentalist sects manage their own affairs without there being any specially paid or trained class who act as ministers, or as the agents of central headquarters. But in Elim the ministry is undoubtedly vital to the continuance of the work in many areas, where in the absence of the ministry other leadership would be difficult to find or insufficient to permit some rotation in office. The Elim church is recruited by organised revival meetings, and it is thus appropriate that those called out should normally be the led and not the leaders

[22] *Elim Evangel*, VII, 1926, No. 1, p. 7.
[23] *Elim Lay Preachers' Handbook*, p. 16.

Elim churches are not mainly a spontaneous demonstration of religious dissatisfaction by people sufficiently able and enterprising to build up a church life for themselves on principles of which they approve; they are a response to a call from a leader, who gathers round him a flock. In the main those drawn into Elim are those who want to hear preachers and not to preach themselves.

The expectation of the movement is to carry its message primarily only to 'ordinary people', that is, to people of no education above the elementary level. During the days when the publishing house was expanding, some of those at headquarters became conscious of the limited market which the movement's literature was experiencing, and sought to induce the membership of the movement to adopt a more educated attitude to the written word. Thus it was that the *Evangel* carried for a considerable time exhortations to members of the movement to read more: 'Keep on Reading'; 'You ought to read'; 'What book have you read this week?' and 'You will soon enjoy reading', supported by suitable scriptural texts such as Isaiah xxxiv, 16, and I Timothy, iv, 13.[24] These slogans in boldest type were not disinterested pleas for members of the movement to educate themselves but clearly had the definite purpose of helping the sales of the publishing house. This fact itself is incidental; what is significant in such a campaign and the style of the slogans is the recognition of the very limited educational background of those in the movement.

Those who have had any education in science or in scientific methods of reasoning, will be, by and large, unlikely converts to a movement of an extreme fundamentalist persuasion. It is again unlikely that the more highly educated members of the community, and the higher social strata, are often sufficiently unreserved and unsophisticated to join readily in a pentecostal meeting, where the ability for emotional display is a distinct advantage.

The cases of members of the Elim movement whose educational background was specifically investigated further confirm the educational limitation common throughout the movement. Almost all had minimal education, and those with further education had had

24 *Elim Evangel*, IX, February 1928. Various issues.

strictly vocational instruction. No one in the group had more than a very rudimentary knowledge of any foreign language, although most had the gift of tongues. None of the younger people, for whom such additional educational exercise might have seemed most profitable, were undertaking any additional educational courses or cultural activities in their leisure time. Indeed, active membership of the Elim movement almost militates against such educational activity; for the young people at least three evenings mid-week are expected to be occupied with church activities, and in some assemblies even more. Education is in no wise normally fostered by the movement, except the study of the Scriptures; in many directions the movement may be said to stand in the way of educational endeavour.

. . . . .

### The Appeal of Pentecostalism—and the Second Generation

Although two dozen interviews establishes no evidence concerning the Elim movement generally, the writer was impressed by the frequency of emotionally disturbed backgrounds among his case studies. Loss of a parent in early life; mixed marriage of the parents, with one a Roman Catholic; immigration to Britain from Ireland and Italy; unhappy home circumstances—were factors present in a number of cases. Almost all had experienced direct answer to prayer, in minor healings or in fulfilment of desires; two of the men had experienced several remarkable visions. The general psychological type appeared obvious from these interviews. Undoubtedly the pentecostal gifts are a distinct source of gratification to some of Elim's members, adding a sense of power and superiority to the feeling of blessedness which being 'born-again' confers. The idea of the new birth and the gaining of the kingdom of heaven is itself attractive to those who have little in this world—wealth, culture, intellect or status. 'No ordinary birth, but only supernatural birth can make us inheritors of the kingdom of God.'[25] Thus worldly values can be denied, for the sake of the greater blessings to be had from the new

[25] *Elim Lay Preachers' Handbook*, p. 75.

birth—a birth into a happier circumstance than the natural birth of the believer. The emphasis in Elim is on 'whosoever will', and on the fact that those who choose are the least and lowliest in the world, not sharing the world's wisdom; but with God they are the saints who will exercise government.

In the assembly the believer, whatever his status outside, stands justified as a 'born-again' believer, and this primary qualification places him among the elect. Here is a circumstance in which the poorest, the most illiterate, the least socially acceptable can, theoretically, and in Elim often in practice command a general social approval—simply by accepting Christ. Many are, nonetheless, still troubled by external afflictions, and by some the end of the world order by cosmic cataclysmic upheaval is more easily conceived than is the death of the self with its subsequent disappearance from that order.

> In thousands of hearts there is a hope. It is the hope of the coming again of the King call [sic] Emmanuel. . . . How often when the pressure of things has become unbearable, the heart has breathed the plaintive cry, 'How long?' And then there has swept over the longing spirit that blessed thought, 'Perhaps to-day'. Is the hunger deeper, and more powerful? Are we prepared for the skyward summons or is our life deeply embedded in the world and its affairs? [26]

Such an expression of hopelessness of this life is not isolated; it is the typical pessimism of the adventist. This is the hope of escaping the misery of life, and of the ending of the world. Such a hope is a sustaining force for those who otherwise might give up a struggle which they find is unequal to their material, social and psychological equipment. These then, are the economically, socially and psychologically underprivileged—or so they might regard themselves but for the transcendent hope they find in their religious faith. That those within the movement are often torn beween the desire to be separate from the world and the desire to have the world's approval is another indication of the compensatory nature of the unique and separate criteria of worthiness which such religious movements

[26] *Elim Evangel*, XXV, 1944, p. 4.

erect. If approval is not to he had on the world's terms, then the sectarian organisation can withdraw and provide its own bases for social worthiness. In another perspective these diverse tendencies represent the denominational and sectarian strains in Elim.

Pentecostal phenomena have a function beyond that of mere release of emotional tensions. These phenomena are themselves a further affirmation of the valuelessness of the things of the world, for they are an evidence of supernatural power which is not to be attained by rank, wealth or intellect, but only through the communion with the Holy Ghost. Spirit gifts are counted as more valuable than anything which the world can offer—and are exclusive to the fellowship and kindred fellowships. The fact that the world makes no demand for such experience does not alter the evaluation, for it is also supernaturally sanctioned. Here again is the compensation for lack of material substance and social position. Pentecostalicm has every reason to appeal to the lower strata of society, the unprivileged and the dispossessed. Thus at an Elim meeting there is something for the emotionally overwrought, and something for the economically and socially disenfranchised. Within the church these gifts further serve to integrate the individual with the group. All the saved are the elect, but the crucial issues are whether a man has received the additional blessing, and is baptised with the Spirit. These become pertinent questions within the group, and prestige is accorded in these terms: 'He is powerfully gifted', 'He has a wonderful gift', 'His is a spirit-filled life', etc. Thus Gee asks, 'Have you received the baptism? Will you receive it? If not you will never become an integral part of the true Pentecostal Revolution, even though you are a member of its local church. You will never be in a position to appreciate its distinctive power and beauty, for that cannot but be reserved for those who share its central reality.' [27]

. . . . .

Elim has no very definite attitude to many social issues, no specific social teaching such as is found in many religious minority

[27] D. Gee, *Why Pentecost?*, 1944, p. 33.

groups. More emphatically sectarian groups often have far more stringent and objectively-prescribed requirements. This lack in itself may weaken the transmission not only of social attitudes in Elim, but even of the specifically religious content of Elim faith. The inculcation of specific responses to various events and circumstances in life itself establishes a discipline and provides a daily regimen which confirms the individual in his own mind in his identification with a particular faith or sect. A set of attitudes are ingrained and the individual left in no doubt about the behaviour which will meet approval among those who constitute his immediate society; the faith is supplemented by a way of life objectively given. In Elim it is the subjective aspects of religious life which receive special emphasis. It is the personal 'born-again' experience, not the obedience to codes and precepts, which is really vital to the individual's acceptance in the church. Together with the idea of the baptism of the Holy Ghost, this remains as the most significant aspect of Elim faith, and neither of these is directly reliant on the movement as such. Even the Elim communion table is not restricted to Elim people—it is open to any 'born-again' believer. By extension it must be accepted that any believer could derive the same benefit from the performance in any evangelical church. All this makes difficult the inculcation in the second generation of a sense of separated unique righteousness in which he must share for his own eternal well-being. Thus it is perhaps not so surprising to find that in a city where Elim has had a church for twenty years there are no second-generation adherents.

Yet there is no lack of young people in Elim. Adolescence is the great age of religious conversion, and it is by such conversion that Elim has grown. The strains under which the adolescent finds himself in our society, the bewildering conflicts of bodily urges and social demands; the dilemma of status; the changes of rôle and responsibility—all lead to doubt concerning behaviour. These conflicts render the young susceptible to profound emotional experience, which a movement like Elim can direct and canalise, and to some extent relieve. The guilt feelings in the period following puberty are accommodated in the teaching of sin, which requires no specific behaviour to warrant its employment. The frustrations of these years can be laid to the charge of the world and the ephemeral nature of its pleasures; pessimism and doubt can be rationalised into the hopelessness of this world, and mitigated by the adventist or eschatological hope. The identification of the individual with Jesus, the martyred son, cannot be entirely overlooked in a religion so profoundly Jesucentric as Elim. This faith has much to offer young people, and it is hardly surprising that they are numerous in Elim's following. They are usually people whose own needs have been met by conversion to Elim, rather than people who have inherited this denominational allegiance. They are not, apparently, recruited in great measure from the Sunday schools supported by the Elim movement. The children in the Elim Sunday schools appear often to include a very large proportion of children of the district as well as the children of Elim members. Elim ministers do not usually expect a very high proportion of Sunday school scholars to be recruited into the church.

Thus we can say that the type of people in the Elim movement are lower class, predominantly women, and include a sizeable proportion of young people. Membership is often not very stable in this movement, and the collapse of Elim churches, and the persistence of Elim evangelism, now meeting with diminished marginal returns, indicates that there is a large proportion of the movement's total membership which is subject to rapid turnover.

## Suggestions for Further Reading

JOHN HIGHET, *The Churches in Scotland Today* (Glasgow: Jackson Son, 1950). This study covers a larger field than *Sects and Society* and therefore gives less detail about each of the organizations referred to. Nevertheless, because of its emphasis on the teachings of the different religious bodies in Scotland it provides interesting comparisons with Wilson's study.

CLIFFORD S. HILL, *West Indian Migrants and the London Churches* (London: Oxford University Press, 1963). Another minority group is given broad treatment in this study, which is interesting because it brings out the difficulties of such a group within a church organization which has not been modified sufficiently to cope with the problems of an underprivileged group with a different skin color and a different cultural background from the existing membership.

CANON K. WARD, *Priests and People* (Liverpool: Liverpool University Press, 1961). The subject of Ward's research was a single Roman Catholic parish in Liverpool; and the relationships between the priest and his parishioners and their membership and participation in church and parish organizations were picked out for special concern. The teaching of the church is accorded scant attention, and in this respect the beliefs of the people interviewed cannot be compared with those of sect members in *Sects and Society*. However, since the Liverpool Catholics are an underprivileged minority, some of the contrasts are revealing.

# ⊸Power in Co-operatives

G. N. OSTERGAARD AND A. H. HALSEY

*Britain is a democracy. However much differences in economic and social interests and differences in attitude toward tradition and change may divide the people, the political constitution emphasizes a government which is responsible to them through their elected representatives. Britain is also a pluralistic society, in the sense that a number of voluntary organizations stand as intermediaries between its population of fifty million people and the government. Two major political parties and five or six minor ones act in this capacity with respect to the election of Members of Parliament. In addition there are many other kinds of voluntary bodies, putting pressure on the government and in various ways making the will of sections of the electorate known to those in power. How effective are they in the twentieth century? Sociologists along with political scientists have sought ways of measuring the degree of political apathy in the population as a preliminary to understanding its nature and grappling with its significance.*

*The study of democratic participation in a population of fifty million people is no simple matter; and an interesting departure was taken in America in 1949 when Seymour Martin Lipset began his study of the International Typographical Union as a kind of micro-*

SOURCE: G. N. Ostergaard and A. H. Halsey, *Power in Co-operatives: A Study of the Internal Politics of British Retail Societies*, Chapter 3 (pp. 67–101). Copyright © 1965 by Basil Blackwell and Mott. Reprinted by permission.

*cosm of a two-party system in a democratic body.*[1] Power in Co-operatives *is another such study, using cooperative retail societies rather than a trade union as the focus of inquiry. The coverage is broader than in Lipset's* Union Democracy *since in 1955 there were about 900 cooperative retail societies in Britain.*[2] *All these societies were asked to complete a questionnaire on their system of government, degree of member participation, etc., and 101 of them with 20,000 members or more were asked to complete a further questionnaire in 1960. At the same time a detailed analysis was made of the formal organization of democracy in these societies as accounted for in their rule books. Ostergaard and Halsey also undertook special inquiries into the conduct of individual societies for specific purposes, such as the degree and nature of pressure group activity, and in one case, as reported in the following selection, a sample of activists and nonactivists was interviewed in 1958.*

*Cooperative retail societies, it should be understood, are organized as businesses selling as broad a range of goods as will generally be found in retail distribution. Anyone may shop at a cooperative retail store, and anyone over the age of sixteen may join a society. This entitles him to receive a dividend on the money he spends with the society during a trading period, usually calculated on a six-month basis. Full membership, however, is not granted unless he also purchases a share in the society, or waits until his dividend has accumulated to make such a purchase automatic. Such full membership carries with it, not only the right to attend business meetings of the society which are open to all members, but also the power to elect the committee of management and other comparable official bodies, and to stand for election himself, subject to such rules and regulations which govern these elections. Each member is allowed one vote irrespective of the number of shares held in the society, so that the*

---

[1] S. M. Lipset, M. A. Trow, and J. S. Coleman, *Union Democracy* (Glencoe: Free Press, 1956). See also S. M. Lipset, *Political Man* (London: Heinemann, 1960), part IV.

[2] At the end of 1965 the number had been reduced by mergers to 740, and at the end of 1966 to 680.

*advantage of holding more than one share is only the fixed interest on shares which is paid every year.*

*Because a cooperative retail society is a much more open voluntary and democratic organization than a trade union, the Ostergaard and Halsey study has wider implications than are valid from* Union Democracy. *At the same time the authors emphasize the significance of objective measures of participation—trading with the society, attending meetings, and voting in elections—and rely on their interview inquiry only to supplement what they discovered from the analysis of these measures. In view of the considerable development of scaling and other devices for studying subjective opinions and attitudes in recent years, they may be criticized for using rather crude indices based on simple questions for this part of their research. Nevertheless, as an example of how far it is possible to take substantive data in the examination of a problem,* Power in Co-operatives *has few equals.*

Apart from its undoubted success as a large and viable organization for the distribution of economic goods, the Co-operative Movement, because of the principles on which it is based, must always face judgment on its status as a democracy. . . . The formal structure of Co-operative government has already been shown to be one of a thoroughgoing democratic character with officers elected by an open membership, on the principle of "one member, one vote". Here we shall examine the extent to which members take advantage of the opportunities open to them and we shall examine the problem of apathy in the context of Co-operative organization.

The question of member participation is crucial not only to an analysis of the working of the Co-operative Movement itself, but also to an understanding of the part played by private organizations in the maintenance of national democracy. . . . Lively participation in democratic private organizations which are independent of state power acts as a barrier against totalitarian movements. Such participation constitutes the mechanism for the recruitment and political education of political men. It provides training in democratic action and access to a forum of oppositional ideas, the toleration and dissemination of which are essential to democratic government. It offers a varied set of opportunities for the nurture and expression of politically and publicly directed energy. Democratic associations constitute the great intermediary foci of loyalties which distinguish the civil from the mass society in which nothing stands between the attachment of a man to his family and to the nation state.

In this general sense the Co-operative Movement has played a significant historical role in the development of British democratic institutions. The origins of democratic forms of association may be traced in the ancient and medieval city. But the modern form of large-scale democracy derives more directly from urban industrialism. The English industrial city of the nineteenth century, growing up around the impulse of capitalistic organization and outside the traditional forms of life in both town and country, challenged the inventiveness of the new proletariat to develop forms of social adaptation capable of mitigating the novel horrors of industrial life. Together with the Trade Unions and the political movements which led eventually to the formation of the Labour Party, the Co-operative store offered protective participation in associations extending beyond the confines of kinship. Just as the Unions fought to secure the rights of men as producers, so the Co-operatives sought to close the circle of economic protection for workers and their families by providing a non-exploitative democracy for consumers.

Of course the working practices of consumer Co-operation, which emerged in the second half of the nineteenth century, were narrow and "economic" by comparison with the early, all-embracing Utopian aims of Owenite Co-operation. Nevertheless, the spirit of the earlier forms, in which the ultimate aim was to transform the competitive basis of capitalist society into a Co-operative Commonwealth, remained, under circumstances which excluded the majority from direct membership in the national polity, as a powerful incentive to participation in a local co-operative democracy. The "comprehensive" aims of Co-operation, which were embraced by the

Rochdale Pioneers, were "to proceed to arrange the powers of production, distribution, education and government, or in other words
to establish a self-supporting home colony of united interests . . .".
These aims at an all embracing transformation of the structure of
society gradually receded before the "segmental" principles of consumer Co-operation advocated by J. T. Mitchell. Nevertheless, the
pull towards participation was certainly enhanced by the wider satisfactions to be gained from Co-operative enfranchisement for the nationally unenfranchised and by the further hopes of a way towards
a more noble, more moral society.

In any case the circumstances of the urban working classes, at
least until the Second World War, were such that even a *consumer*
Co-operative theory could be liberally interpreted. While citizenship
carried with it minimal social rights in a society as yet uncommitted
to "Welfare" and unable to provide affluence for the mass of the
population, social securities had to be sought privately. The services
of the Co-operatives, or at least the more imaginative and energetic
among them, were correspondingly comprehensive and highly
valued. Thus, even to-day a Co-operative member may be able to
recall his youthful experience in terms of participation in an almost
total community. "All our wants, or at least all our needs, could be
supplied, for besides the many branches like that at Hill Street, there
were central shops for tailoring, drapery, footwear, furniture and
even a department for undertaking. . . . Best of all from my point
of view was the newsroom . . . furnished with the dailies and popular monthly magazines. . . . Education in its stricter sense was
served by the provision of scholarships awarded by examination for
members' children every year. . . . Yes, all of us—men, women and
children alike—were well looked after by the Old Co-op. It could
feed, clothe, shelter (by providing a mortgage for house purchase)
and in the end, bury us. Even in his last journey the true co-operator
brought 'divi' as well as death payment to those left behind." [3]

To-day, however, though still the most thoroughgoing form of

[3] T. W. Pateman, "Shopping at the Co-op", *Manchester Guardian,* 28th May,
1958.

private democracy in industrial society, the Co-operative is widely thought of as deprived of its democratic substance through the apathy of its members. This problem is not a new one.[4] But the sociological and psychological conditions which fostered high rates of member participation in the private welfare society of the industrial worker have undergone radical transformations, especially since the First World War. What is the extent and how serious is the significance of this "crisis of apathy" in the Co-operative Movement at the present day?

Two preliminary points may be emphasized. First, despite the stress laid on participation in voluntary associations for the maintenance of democracy and the resistance of "mass society" and despite the traditional characterization of Britain and America as nations of joiners, there is ample evidence from recent research that membership of voluntary associations does not loom large in the lives of ordinary men and women. The fact is that, for the majority, social life in industrial society, as in societies with a less complex division of labour, is largely contained within the primary group memberships of kinship and neighbourhood, and the attachment of the individual to the wider organizations of society is formed and maintained through passive connection to the mass media of communication. Active public participation is characteristic only of a small minority.

Second, there is the question of the meaning of participation in a Co-operative. Our purpose is to gauge the active degree of adherence by members to the aims of the Co-operative Movement. We seek, in other words, a measure of motivation towards goals or ideals which are multiple, imprecisely defined and subject to change over time. The significance of the actual measures available to us is open to varied interpretation. Active participation in the affairs of a society may derive from Co-operative zeal or from motivations unconnected with Co-operative principles. A man may seek office in his

---

[4] In their *The Consumers' Co-operative Movement*, 1921, the Webbs refer to the apathy of members as "the gravest remediable shortcoming of the present Co-operative movement" (p. 305).

society as a means of securing recognition or position in his Union, a political party or the local community. Attendance at a meeting may be motivated only by interest in the size of the dividend. On the other hand, failure to contest elections may result not from apathy but from satisfaction with the current management of affairs. When all appears to be going well with his Co-operative, a member may feel no need to participate actively: when things appear to be going badly, however, such a member may well find himself impelled to take a more active part. Clearly, the knowledge that there are, or may be, such "foul weather" members may influence leaders in their general policies. This point and the fact that Co-operatives are voluntary associations in which in the last resort members may "vote with their feet", should be borne in mind in interpreting the findings of our study. Participation and democracy, although connected, are not the same thing. The constitution of a Co-operative remains democratic even though only a tiny minority participates and the ultimate power lies with the members even if they do not normally exercise it. The crucial test is the extent of the influence wielded by the members over those who actually exercise authority and this cannot be measured merely in terms of participation figures.

## Measures of Participation

On the basis of available information we may use three measures of member participation—trading, attendance at members' meetings and voting in societies' elections. The first of these is related to the "segmental" goal of Co-operation, i.e., to the society as a retail trading association, and is therefore minimal in that it could be applied to measure the loyalty of individuals to any type of retail enterprise.

In Table 1 we show trends in the trading "loyalty" of Co-operative members as indicated by the average annual sales per member in the retail societies. There can be no doubt as to the general trend. It seems that, adjusting for price changes, the average sales per member rose up to the 1890s, but since that time there has been continuous

*Table 1. Average Sales Per Member in Co-operative Societies, from 1881*

| YEAR | TOTAL MEMBERSHIP | RETAIL SALES PER MEMBER ( £ ) | | | | |
|------|------|------|------|------|------|------|
| | Thousands | Unadjusted | Corrected for changes in price level | | | |
| | | | (a) | (b) | (c) | (d) |
| | | £ | £ | £ | £ | £ |
| 1881 | 547 | 28.2 | 20.1 | | | |
| 1890 | 960 | 28.0 | 26.4 | | | |
| 1900 | 1,703 | 29.3 | 29.3 | 29.3 | | |
| 1910 | 2,529 | 28.3 | | 25.9 | 22.0 | |
| 1914 | 3,054 | 28.8 | | 24.7 | 24.7 | |
| 1920 | 4,460 | 56.4 | | | 18.9 | |
| 1930 | 6,856 | 33.9 | | | 19.7 | |
| 1940 | 8,717 | 34.3 | | | 18.0 | 31.32(e) |
| 1950 | 10,692 | 57.41 | | | | 26.01 |
| 1960 | 12,957 | 79.71 | | | | 25.28 |

(a) Adjusted by Old Board of Trade Retail Food Index (1900 = 100). Based on nine articles in London.

(b) Adjusted by Revised Board of Trade Retail Food Index (1900 = 100). Based on prices of thirty-three articles in London.

(c) Adjusted by Ministry of Labour Retail Food Index (1914 = 100, transposed to base 1900 = 100). Based on prices in all parts of Great Britain.

(d) Adjusted on basis of 1938 prices.

(e) This figure refers to 1938.

SOURCES: G. D. H. Cole, *A Century of Co-operation*, 1944, p. 375. *Co-operative Review*, September 1961, p. 307.

decline. In 1943 Cole estimated the decline at one-third.[5] In the last twenty years average sales per member have fallen off by a further sixth. Nor is this the most stringent measure of trading loyalty. In 1880 the average sale per member of £28 represented something like one-third of the income of a typical member, whereas the present figure of £80 probably represents at best about one-tenth of the average member's earnings.

The same general trend emerges from the records of member

[5] G. D. H. Cole, *A Century of Co-operation*, 1944, p. 376.

holdings of share and loan capital. These are summarized for the period since 1938 in Table 2. When price adjustments are made to allow for the decline in the real value of the pound it appears that the average holding of the Co-operative member has been reduced to a third of the 1938 level—and this in a period of unprecedented advance in the affluence of the mass of the British population. According to a recent survey of share holding "it would appear that more than 50 per cent. of the Co-operative membership may have nothing more than a nominal share capital holding of £1 or £2. Thus six or seven million may be in this position. Nearly three-quarters or more of the total membership may not have a larger capital holding than £10." [6] It is clear from these figures for capital and expenditure that Co-operative members have a low and declining economic attachment to their societies.

The other two measures of member participation—attendance at meetings and voting in Co-operative elections—bring us a little nearer to assessing identification with the "comprehensive" aims of Co-operation. Nevertheless, the limitations of these indices already mentioned must be re-emphasized and it may be added that they

Table 2. *Average Capital per Member in Co-operative Societies, Since 1938*

| YEAR | SHARE AND LOAN CAPITAL | |
|------|-------|-------------------------|
| | TOTAL | ADJUSTED TO 1938 VALUE |
| | £ | £ |
| 1938 | 21.40 | 21.40 |
| 1945 | 30.13 | 17.02 |
| 1950 | 27.68 | 12.58 |
| 1955 | 24.62 | 8.79 |
| 1959 | 22.83 | 7.30 |

SOURCE: *Co-operative Review,* February 1961, p. 43.

[6] J. A. Hough, "Co-operative Capital and the Member", *Co-operative Review,* February 1961, p. 43.

merely provide measures of the extent of *formal* participation, though in the two most significant aspects of democratic control. They ignore participation in such other aspects of Co-operative government as the election of education committees, and they take no account of any *informal* membership activity, such as participation in "auxiliary" Guild organizations and "pressure groups". However, the available evidence suggests that it is improbable that a more elaborate index including these other activities would alter the picture in any material way.

The most recent figures concerning attendance and voting for the Movement as a whole are those obtained in our national inquiry of 1955. The proportion of ordinary members attending business meetings in that year was found to be 0.5 per cent. and the proportion voting in management committee elections was 1.65 per cent. or one in every sixty members. In absolute terms this means that of the Co-operative Movement's 11¼ million members, not more than 56,000 other than committee members attended business meetings in 1955. Although the proportion voting is higher than the proportion attending, in some respects the voting figures reveal a relatively worse situation, since in no less than 232 out of 533 societies (i.e., 44 per cent.) replying to this question, the management committee election was uncontested. It is not suggested that, in the bulk of these 232 societies, such elections are regularly uncontested (though this is true of some), but there is no reason to believe that the figure of 44 per cent. represents an unusual year. In other words, although the same societies may not be included in the uncontested group from one year to the next, it is probable that no more than three-fifths of all retail society management committee elections are contested at the present time.

As with the economic indices, the trend over time seems to be towards reduced participation. Before our survey in 1955 the accepted figure for attendance was 2 per cent. In 1960 we repeated the 1955 survey for all societies with a membership of 20,000 or more in the earlier year. For these societies the attendance in 1955 had been 0.31 per cent.: by 1960 it had fallen to 0.23 per cent. The comparable figures for voting in Board elections were 1.63 per cent. and 1.41 per cent. respectively. Thus, in the five years 1955–60, attendance diminished proportionately by one-quarter and voting by one-eighth. Of course, total membership rose in the same period; but looking at absolute figures for the 97 societies from which we have statistics for both years, the aggregate number attending decreased from 20,522 to 17,546; and the voters decreased from 109,341 to 105,508. In short, the record of participation in the democratic control of Co-operatives is one of *diminuendo* on small numbers.

We may add final emphasis to these indices of apathy by comparing them with the participation rates in other private organizations. The Co-operatives have never succeeded in capturing the trading loyalty of the consumer. Non-Co-operative forms of retail trade continue to dominate the market. The most comparable type of retail organization—multiples and departmental stores—command a quarter of the trade compared with the Co-operative one-tenth, and the remaining two-thirds falls to the competitive private trader. Comparison with private economic enterprise in terms of capital holding is ruled out by the difference in the social composition between the two types of enterprise. Nevertheless, the figures presented in Table 2 are sufficient to show that the majority do not belong to the Movement effectively as owners.

With regard to attendance at meetings there appear to be no organizations with such low rates of member participation as those prevailing in the British retail societies. Poor attendance at the meetings of voluntary societies is not in itself surprising and as Lipset and his colleagues remark in their discussion of the ITU it is more useful to ask why the minority attends rather than why the majority stays away. The typical Co-operative meeting is no exception. It is usually an unexciting affair and is comprehensible only to those who have become familiar with the technicalities of retail trading, the management of accounts and the details of activities among Co-operative auxiliary bodies. Only occasionally will the fireworks of political or public debate intrude to enliven the proceedings for the inexpert attender. Nevertheless, for all that, comparison again suggests an exceptionally low attendance. . . . Thus in a book intended to dramatize the parlous condition of member participation in the Transport and General Workers' Union Joseph Goldstein calculated branch meeting attendance at 4 per cent. for the years 1942–47.[7] He concluded that "no evidence has been discovered on Branch attendance in the TGWU which in any way refutes the clear cut impression of apathy. . . . It therefore becomes impossible to avoid the conclusion that the Branch meeting—if not the Branch itself—as an institution designed to elicit wide-scale member participation has failed to fulfil its function." [8] The implication for the functioning of the average Co-operative society, with participation rates of about one-eighth of those quoted for the TGWU, is depressingly obvious.

Comparative voting statistics lead again to the same conclusion. The range of participation runs from a high point in national elections (democratic and totalitarian) to a low point among the British Co-operatives. The British General Election of 1959 had a turn-out of 78.7 per cent. Birch gives just under 40 per cent. for County Council elections and 49 to 55 per cent. for municipal elections.[9] Goldstein calculated that "in eighty elections held between 1937 and 1947 for territorial representatives to the General Executive Council of the TGWU, an average of 37 per cent of the total eligible membership voted".[10] In a recent Finnish Co-operative election the figure was 35 per cent. The figure for British Co-operatives in 1960 of 1.41 per cent. is therefore at the lowest extremity of membership apathy.

## Causes and Correlates of Apathy

We are thus forced to the conclusion that, whatever view we take of the importance of member participation to the maintenance of democracy, the vast majority of Co-operative members in 1964 participate only as uncommitted shoppers and hardly at all as political members of a voluntary democracy. Moreover, the contem-

[7] J. Goldstein, *The Government of a British Trade Union,* Allen and Unwin, 1952.
[8] *Ibid.,* p. 202.
[9] A. Birch, *Small Town Politics,* OUP, 1959, p. 97.
[10] J. Goldstein, op. cit., p. 99.

porary conditions of widespread apathy are the low point of a secular decline of activism in the Co-operative Movement from its beginnings among urban industrial workers in the nineteenth century. In the course of a century of developing industrialism the pull of Co-operative participation has been gradually enfeebled.

The industrial worker in 1850 was virtually propertyless; his income was low and insecure; he had no national vote and no party to represent him; he was cut off from the middle and upper classes and could not see reasonable hopes for self-betterment either for himself or his children, either through business success or education. In his daily life he was surrounded by men of the same occupation and the same life-chances: this was the social world—a world of constricted kin and class horizons—within which he had to seek his securities and his opportunities. The Co-operative as a private welfare society was, under these circumstances, a powerful magnet to the energies of the politically and socially aspirant. It offered not only food, clothes and shelter, but education and the prospect of political and social transformation of capitalist society. Indeed, it was the *only* social movement with such comprehensive aims in the nineteenth century. As such, and before the rise of syndicalism and state socialism, it could command the whole attention of those who aspired to work for total transformation of capitalist society. Moreover, besides having social conditions and social aims calculated to maximize participation among enthusiasts, the Co-operative was typically of a size and complexity that fitted naturally with the boundaries of acquaintance set by kin and neighbourhood for the industrial worker. The societies were typically tiny. In 1881 the average number of members in a society was 564.

The potential Co-operator to-day faces a wholly different situation. He is better off, nationally enfranchised and supported by a considerable apparatus of state-provided benefits. His environment is no longer homogeneous and isolated by class or occupation; he lives on a housing estate of more or less mixed composition and, accurately or not, he sees the world of opportunity and success as open to his children through education. He does not need the Co-operative to satisfy his aspirations—economic, political or social. Meanwhile the Co-operative Movement as the movement of radical social transformation has disappeared. "Segmental" rather than "comprehensive" aims guide its policies and even the aims of consumer Co-operation . . . have been narrowly and unimaginatively interpreted by many societies.

At the same time the typical organization of a Co-operative has developed enormous scale and complexity with all that this implies in the way of impersonality and bureaucracy. In 1962 there were 826 societies with a total membership of just over 13 million; but rather more than a third of all the members were accounted for by the nineteen societies with over 100,000 members in each. By contrast in 1900 there were many more societies (1,439), but typically much smaller in size, so that the total membership (1,707,000) was less than one-eighth of what it is to-day. At the present time more than half of the Co-operative members are in societies having a membership of more than 50,000: in 1900 there was not a single society of this size.

This explanation of the secular drift towards apathy is reinforced by the pattern of variation among societies in relation to attendance and voting. Thus size is the outstanding correlate of apathy (see Table 3). Participation tends to decline, proportionately the larger the society. In our 1955 survey, among the ten responding societies having 100,000 or more members the average attendance at business meetings was 0.27 per cent.; for the sixty-eight societies with a membership of 20,000–50,000 it was 0.4 per cent., and for societies with less than 1,000 members the percentage was 3.06.

This trend raises the question of the possible incompatibility of business efficiency and democratic control. It may be that part of the price of increased efficiency through amalgamation may be a concomitant increase in member apathy and hence a weakening of Co-operative democracy unless new means can be found to evoke active member participation in the larger society. Of course, size alone does not explain the distribution of apathy. Barnsley British is in the 100,000+ group, yet it returned the highest "voting performance" in 1955—10.27 per cent. in a range which descended to 0.17 per cent. This kind of variation must be sought in factors peculiar to

*Table 3. Attendance at Meetings by Size of Co-operative Society in 1955*

| MEMBERSHIP | NO. OF SOCIETIES RESPONDING | TOTAL MEMBERSHIP | PERCENTAGE ATTENDING |
|---|---|---|---|
| 100,000+ | 10 | 2,858,652 | 0.27 |
| 50,001–100,000 | 24 | 1,795,806 | 0.28 |
| 20,001–50,000 | 67 | 2,133,216 | 0.40 |
| 10,001–20,000 | 84 | 1,168,692 | 0.53 |
| 5,001–10,000 | 95 | 694,873 | 0.81 |
| 3,001–5,000 | 84 | 330,255 | 0.93 |
| 2,001–3,000 | 51 | 126,879 | 1.20 |
| 1,001–2,000 | 65 | 95,909 | 1.23 |
| 1,000 or less | 69 | 42,747 | 3.06 |
| Total | 549 | 9,247,079 | 0.43 |

individual societies. Thus Barnsley has a high level of Guild activity and advertising of candidates while Sherburn Hill, where voting reached 35.95 per cent. in 1960, operates a postal ballot.

The trends in social and economic conditions to which we have appealed as explaining the secular decline in member participation appear also to be reflected in participation statistics for the different regions of the country. Thus in the South, Midlands and South-West, where industry tends to be newer and more heterogeneous, the population more mobile and prosperous and the Co-operative societies larger, the rates of attendance tend to be lower than in the areas of more traditional working-class industrial life in Scotland, Wales and Northern England. To take one example, the society with the highest rate of attendance (62 per cent.) in 1955 was a very small society, situated in a close knit, homogeneous Welsh community of slate quarriers at Llanrug.

## Co-operative Co-partnerships

The retail societies are based on a consumer theory of Co-operation. It may therefore be instructive to compare their membership participation with that in producer Co-operatives. To this end we surveyed all societies affiliated to the Co-operative Productive Federation in 1956. The returns showed that 10.2 per cent. of the total membership had attended the last business meeting. Voting statistics showed that in eleven out of the twenty-six responding societies the most recent election had been uncontested. Counting all the members in these societies the proportion of the total membership voting in 1956 was 8.5 per cent. In a few of the eleven societies there had been no contest for several years. The remainder, however, were able to provide figures for recently contested elections and using these, the aggregate percentage of voters rises to 14.5 per cent. Variations in attendance ran from 2.5 per cent. to 97.4 per cent. and in voting in contested elections from 6.2 per cent. to 66.7 per cent.

The inverse correlation between size and participation which we saw among the retail societies also obtains among the co-partnerships as may be seen from Table 4. In this case, it should be noticed, the relationship exists despite a much smaller range in the size of societies.

*Table 4. Attendance of Members and Size of Society among Co-operative Co-partnerships*

| SIZE GROUP | NUMBER OF SOCIETIES | TOTAL MEMBERSHIP | PERCENTAGE ATTENDING |
|---|---|---|---|
| Under 100 | 6 | 416 | 38.9 |
| 100–249 | 7 | 1,122 | 21.4 |
| 250–499 | 7 | 2,327 | 12.1 |
| 500–999 | 4 | 2,376 | 8.3 |
| 1,000+ | 3 | 4,318 | 4.6 |
| All | 27 | 10,559 | 10.2 |

However, the most interesting analysis of participation in co-partnerships is in relation to types of member. Although the co-partnership form of Co-operation is distinguished by the provision of an element of worker or producer control, there are in fact four types of member; workers in the enterprise; Co-operative societies, mainly retail but also other co-partnership societies; individuals, mainly ex-employees and their relatives and (in about half of the societies) trade unions. The distribution of the membership between these four types in the 25 societies providing detailed information appears in Table 5.

*Table 5. Attendances and Types of Member*

| TYPE OF MEMBER (1) | NUMBER OF MEMBERS (2) | PERCENTAGE OF TOTAL MEMBERSHIP (3) | PERCENTAGE OF TOTAL ATTENDING (4) | PERCENTAGE OF MEMBERS ATTENDING (5) |
|---|---|---|---|---|
| Workers | 2,595 | 30.2 | 67.5 | 25.9 |
| Co-op. Socs. | 2,519 | 29.4 | 9.9 | 3.9 |
| Individuals | 3,434 | 40.0 | 21.7 | 6.3 |
| Trade Unions | 36 | 0.4 | 0.9 | 25.0 |
| Total | 8,584 | 100.0 | 100.0 | — |

It will be seen that, whereas the workers constitute only 30 per cent. of the total membership, they constitute by far the largest proportion of attenders (67.5 per cent.). This contrasts markedly with the position of Co-operative societies which constitute roughly the same proportion of the total membership but provide just under 10 per cent. of the attenders. Comparing columns 3 and 4, it appears that, in relation to their proportionate total membership workers and, to a much lesser degree, trade unions are "over-represented" at business meetings, while Co-operative societies and individuals are "under-represented". Clearly, the degree of effective worker control in co-partnerships is greater than might be expected from the membership distribution figures.

These aggregate figures should not, however, be taken to imply that the worker members are dominant in *every* society. An examination in detail shows that in six of the twenty-five societies the workers were in a minority at the business meeting. Nevertheless, the general impression of worker control remains. In only five of these societies do the workers constitute a majority of the member-ship, but in nineteen instances they had a majority at the business meeting. In two societies all those who attended were workers and in nine others over 80 per cent. of the attenders were workers.

Worker dominance is, of course, a direct result of worker in-terest. Column 5 in Table 5 shows that workers *as a group* are more interested than other types of member, although it is notable that trade union members, in proportion to their numbers, are a close second. Despite the fact that they hold over 40 per cent. of the total share capital. Co-operative societies appear as the least interested type of member. The aggregate figure of 25.9 per cent. participation by workers as a group masks variations as between societies. Detailed examination shows that in ten out of twenty-five societies more than 50 per cent. of the worker members attended, while in two instances there was a 100 per cent. attendance of the members in this category. In only one instance each did more than 50 per cent. of the society and individual members attend.

The voting figures repeat the pattern for attendance. In elections, the worker members are dominant, with individual members second, Co-operative societies third, and trade unions fourth. In terms of interest in elections *as a group*, workers are again in the lead, fol-lowed by trade unions, individuals and Co-operative societies in that order.

An explanation of the relatively greater degree of interest shown by worker members is not hard to find. Most business meetings are held on the premises of the societies and frequently during working time or immediately after. It therefore requires less effort on the part of such members to attend and vote. Also, the tradition of workers' control in Co-operative co-partnerships no doubt tends to discourage more active participation by other types of member. It is part of the established expectation of members that in most societies the worker element will be dominant.

It is improbable, however, that ease of access to meetings and the force of tradition account wholly for the greater interest shown by worker members. An underlying factor is that the association of men as producers evokes a more active interest than most other types of association, including associations of consumers. In a very real sense a man's relation to his work is more fundamental than his other social relations. It involves more of his time and energies and his position in society is largely dependent upon his occupational role. He is likely, therefore, to be more active in associations involving his work than in associations concerned with consumption or leisure time activities.

Certainly this factor helps to explain why the level of participation is higher in Co-operative co-partnerships than in retail societies. In view of the size factor it is not, of course, possible to compare the overall participation figures in the two types of Co-operative. The appropriate figure to compare with the 10.2 per cent, attendance in co-partnerships is not the 0.5 per cent. for all retail societies, but the figure of 1.8 per cent. for retail societies of 2,000 or less members. The difference is then smaller, but remains striking. No advocate of Co-operative co-partnership will be satisfied with a participation figure of 10 per cent., but at least it provides some justification for opposition to those who identify Co-operation with exclusive control by consumers. There are many grounds for supporting the principles of Co-operative co-partnership, but not least among them is that they provide the basis for a more effective democracy than is to be found elsewhere in the Co-operative Movement.

## The Activists

Our discussion of member participation has shown that the reality of democratic practice in the Co-operative Movement depends upon a tiny minority of activists. Who are they? How far do they represent the main body of inactive members? We may begin by asking what kinds of people serve on the Management Boards of the societies.

The "Co-op" is by tradition a working-class institution and one moreover in which day to day participation by the working-class family rests mainly on the housewife. A survey of a random sample of the adult population of England and Wales comprising 6,821 persons and carried out in 1945, showed that 51 per cent. were either themselves members of the Co-operative Movement or were connected with it through a member of their immediate family, usually the housewife. However, the extent of membership was uneven as between different social strata, as may be seen from Table 6.

*Table 6. Membership of Co-operative Retail Societies by Occupational Group, 1945*

| OCCUPATIONAL GROUP | PER CENT. OF GROUP IN MEMBERSHIP |
|---|---|
| Professional classes, salaried executive workers, etc. | 25 |
| Proprietors of shops or businesses, including farmers | 23 |
| Salaried clerical workers | 37 |
| Factory and other heavy industrial workers, transport workers, etc. | 53 |
| Miners | 67 |
| Agricultural workers | 32 |
| All other weekly wage earners, including low grade clerical workers | 41 |
| Retired and unoccupied (including old age pensioners) | 37 |

Membership is biased heavily towards the urban industrial workers and the miners and includes only one in four of the professional and business classes.

Our survey of the Management Boards shows, on the other hand, that their social composition, by comparison with the general population, is biased in the opposite direction. They are recruited relatively more heavily from the middle-class than from those in manual employment. Carr-Saunders, Florence and Peers, on the basis of an inquiry in the 1930s, stated that the Boards were "drawn in the main from the skilled artisan class".[11] This is still true, but only just: skilled workers contributed 53 per cent. of the Board

[11] *Consumers' Co-operation in Great Britain,* 1942, p. 87.

members whose occupations or husbands' occupations were reported. The non-manual workers, including substantial numbers of insurance agents, managers of Co-operative branch stores and school teachers, made up 24 per cent., compared with 18 per cent. in the adult population of England and Wales, and the unskilled workers 3 per cent., compared with 13 per cent. for the country as a whole.

The authors of the earlier study go on to say that the Boards are more working-class than the membership on the grounds that, though trading is done with large sections of the middle class, the working-class provide the active Co-operative membership. If this was true then, it is no longer true. Membership of Co-operative societies is heaviest among manual workers, whereas our inquiry clearly establishes that the social composition of the Boards is "superior" to that of the general population.

. . . . .

A further clue to the explanation of this aspect of unrepresentativeness of the Board membership is to be found in the relation between candidature and trading. We know . . . that the more active traders tend also to be more active participants in the affairs of their societies. The average purchases for the preceding week among members who said that they attended quarterly meetings was 35s. 3d., compared with 22s. 10d. among those members who said that they attended no meetings. We also know that both purchasing and shareholding qualifications are required of candidates in Board elections by most societies. It is a reasonable assumption that the better-off members would be those most likely to have high purchases and to meet the shareholding requirement for candidature. In consequence social class or economic position can act as a selective factor raising the chances of election of the middle-class and relatively highly paid skilled workers among the rank and file of the membership.

Nevertheless, as compared with the Boards of Directors of private industry, the Co-operative Boards continue to provide a broad-based opportunity for participation in economic government. In 1936 a random sample of 463 British Companies of all sizes revealed that 8 per cent. of the directorships were held by titled persons.[12] In our survey of the Co-operative Boards we found only one aristocrat. The Co-operative Boards also recruit much more heavily from the working-class than do the Boards of the Nationalized Industries. In 1950 an inquiry showed that, apart from Trade Unionists (16 out of 79), the Nationalized Industry Boards were made up predominantly of company directors, higher civil servants, managers, engineers and other professional people. Of course, we are here comparing large undertakings with small, but if we consider only the 102 presidents of societies with more than 20,000 members among our respondents it turns out that 49 of these are manual workers, 45 are middle-class and 8 unclassified.

Again, of the 277 Labour Members of Parliament elected in 1955, 97 (35 per cent.) were working-class. Recruitment to high position is thus more likely for manual workers on the Co-operative than on the political side of the British working-class movement.

The composition of the Boards is predominantly male. Though the day to day interests of housewives would suggest the Co-operatives as a highly appropriate field of public activity for women, it is in fact the case that the presence of women on the management committees is a recent development and one which is typical of the larger societies only.

The extent of "discrimination" against women can only be judged in terms of their proportion in the membership as a whole. In 1960 we collected information from eighty-eight societies which indicated that about two-thirds of all Co-operative members are women. There is a tendency for the proportion to be higher in the larger societies. If there were no "discrimination" on sex grounds one would expect from those figures that about two-thirds of the Board members would be women. In fact the proportion of women on Boards is one-fifth. In 1955 there were 251 women Board members out of a total of 1,229 in the group of societies studied, i.e., 20.4 per cent.; in 1960 the comparable figures were 258 out of 1,242, i.e., 20.7 per cent. A detailed analysis of the returns, however, shows that

[12] P. Sargant Florence, *The Logic of British and American Industry,* 1953, p. 206.

there was a slight tendency away from sex discrimination. In 1955, 12 per cent. of the societies had no women Board members; in 1960 there were 8 per cent. in this category. This marginal shift in the direction of sex equality is probably accounted for by the size factor. The larger the society the more likely is it that women will be elected to the Board. "Towards the end of the last century, it was unusual for women to take part even in quarterly meetings." [13] The development of women's representation on the Boards owes a great deal to the work of the Women's Guild. Our information shows that Guild activity and women's representation are highly correlated, and, conversely, that the women Board members concentrate their activity heavily on the social rather than the trading affairs of the societies—on education, welfare, guild activities, etc. Thus, for example, the presence of women on a Board tends to increase the education grant or at least to prevent it from being zero.

Women Board members are more usually middle-aged than the men. There are proportionately more men under 50 and over 70: 64 per cent. of the women compared with 50 per cent. of the men are between 50 and 65. The vast majority (83 per cent.) of the women are housewives and our inquiry indicates that they are more representative of the membership than are the men in the sense that they represent a more faithful sample of its population by occupational grade and by type of employment.

However, the typical Board member is an old man with many years of service to the Society. Well over one-third of those serving at the time of our first survey (1955) were over 60, one in five were over the normal retiring age of 65 and more than 8 per cent. were over 70, the legally compulsory retiring age for company directors. Nevertheless, it should be noticed that the situation among private undertakings is, or was, worse. An inquiry in 1933 showed that 57 per cent. of British directors were over 60 and 42 per cent. over 65.

The record of years of service parallels that of the age composition of the Boards. Members usually retire after two years, but are normally eligible for re-election. Indeed, "in some societies it seems to be assumed that the only course which can lead to a member

[13] Carr-Saunders *et al., op. cit.,* p. 88.

leaving the committee is death".[14] Thus no less than 189 out of 521 presidents had served for more than ten years and 14 per cent. for more than twenty years. There can be no doubt that committees recruited in this way will display caution rather than imaginative enterprise and all the signs indicate that "gerontocracy" is becoming an increasingly dominant feature of the Co-operative Movement. On the other hand, it is difficult to see how, given the social composition of the Boards, matters could be otherwise, for the vast majority have an educational and occupational background which precludes the possibility of learning how to direct an economic enterprise except by long experience as a Board member. Experience, under the circumstances, is a necessary substitute for qualification.

Our survey material does permit a direct appraisal of the motives which lead members of Co-operative societies to seek election to Management Boards. In particular it is not possible to judge the strength of idealistic devotion to those principles of Co-operation which traditionally define the ends of the movement. Motivation of this kind should presumably manifest itself in a high incidence of attachment on the part of Co-operators to the Trade Union and political wings of the socialist and working-class movement. Yet only 7 per cent. of those covered by our inquiry were reported as being politically active in the sense of holding office in any kind of political organization. The distribution of this small minority of holders of political office was:

| | |
|---|---|
| Labour and Co-operative Parties | 436 |
| Liberal | 4 |
| Conservative | 4 |
| Communist | 3 |
| Total | 447 |

No doubt the extent of political participation is underestimated by these figures, but there is no reason to suppose that the proportionate distribution between parties is wildly inaccurate. If this is so, then the political balance of the Management Boards is far to the

[14] Carr-Saunders *et al.*, op. cit., p. 87.

left of the rank and file membership and this in turn is to the left of the general population. The distribution of political allegiance of members and non-members in 1945 was as follows:

|  | VOTING INTENTION AT GENERAL ELECTION | | |
| --- | --- | --- | --- |
|  | LABOUR | LIBERAL | CONSERVATIVE |
|  | % | % | % |
| Members of Co-operative Societies | 64.3 | 8.6 | 26.4 |
| Non-members of Co-operative Societies | 41.4 | 13.1 | 44.4 |

We may infer that a left-wing political attitude not only predisposes people to join Co-operative Societies, but also operates within the societies as a selective factor in the recruitment of the Boards. At all events Co-operatives retain that affinity with the Labour Party which they acquired in the first half of the twentieh century, and societies like Leeds are conspicuous mainly because they are politically exceptional.

Rather more than 8 per cent. of the Board members also hold official positions in Trade Unions. In addition about one in four are active in other public affairs; over 5 per cent. are Justices of the Peace, 9 per cent, are in local government and 15 per cent. in other community and social service organizations. Nor is activity within the Co-operative Movement necessarily confined to service on the Management Board: 12.3 per cent. hold official positions on other committees concerned with Co-operative trading, 9 per cent. in Co-operative social organizations such as the Guilds and 6.8 per cent. in the Co-operative Union.

Thus at least a minority of the Board members are public men, active in more than one form of Co-operative, political (usually Socialist), trade union or other community or social service activity.

## Activists and Non-Activists

There is a common impression that activity in Co-operatives is to some extent a family affair; that is to say, that the tradition of being active will be passed on from parent to child. If there is substance in this view, one would expect that present members whose parents belonged to a Co-operative would be more likely than others to be active. Our survey of one Society in 1958 [Ten Acres and Stirohley Co-operative Society] supports this hypothesis. A majority of both activists and ordinary members had parents who were or had been Co-operators, but the proportion was higher among the activists (69 per cent. as against 58 per cent.). There is also a strong tendency for activity to be a family affair in another sense. Forty-four per cent. of the activists compared with only 6 per cent. of the general membership had husbands or wives who were also members of the Society.

More significant than the simple family connection, however, is the connection a member may have to his society either as an employee or as a relative of an employee. Respondents were asked whether they themselves or any of their relatives were employed by the Society or any neighbouring Co-operative, including federal undertakings such as the Co-operative Wholesale Society. Twenty-four per cent. of the activists were either so employed or married to an employee. When relatives were included, this proportion rose to 41 per cent. These figures contrast markedly with those for the ordinary members, only 1 per cent. of whom were employees, although a further 16 per cent had relatives who were employees. To put it in another way, one out of every four TASCOS activists had a strong employee connection and two out of five had an employee connection of some kind. Less than one in five of the ordinary members, however, had any employee connection and this was mainly of the weaker (relative employed) kind. Moreover, in the case of the activists, the employee connection was mainly at the managerial rather than at the rank-and-file employee level. Ten per cent. of the activists were either themselves managers or the wives of managers, and a further 2.5 per cent. had relatives employed at this level.

By definition, activists have a different relation to their society than do ordinary members. In an effort to clarify this relation, respondents were asked what sort of reasons made them join the

Society. The answers to such a question cannot strictly be interpreted as providing the actual reasons for joining since memories may be faulty or the real motives may be hidden from the respondents. Nevertheless, they do reveal something of the member's relation with, and attitude to his society. As might be expected, the reasons given by respondents were varied. Reasons connected with family tradition ranked high for both activists and ordinary members. 22.5 per cent, and 28 per cent, respectively gave answers of the kind: "Grew up with the idea", "My mother was a satisfied member so I joined when I got married". Apart from this category of reasons, there were marked differences between the two groups; broadly, the responses of the ordinary members referred to the Co-operative as a trading organization, while the responses of the activists showed a high degree of ideological commitment to the Co-operative Movement. Forty-one per cent. of the ordinary members mentioned the dividend, 37 per cent. the quality of goods or services offered, and 33 per cent. convenience of the shops.[15] In contrast, while 21 per cent. of the activists mentioned the dividend, 55 per cent. gave reasons which were clearly ideological, e.g., "The Co-op. is an organization which gives consumers a chance", "Because it is a working-class movement", and "The profits go to the consumer not the capitalist". 12.5 per cent. of the activists also mentioned the social and educational activities of the Society, and a further 11 per cent. gave reasons involving their employee connection. Not a single ordinary member responded in terms of ideology, educational activities or employment.

On the assumption that the dividend would rank high among reasons given for joining, a further question was asked: "Would you continue to shop at the Co-op if it didn't give a dividend? Why is that?" The question is, of course, hypothetical and the replies are not necessarily a good guide to what the members would do if they were in fact faced with the situation. But again, the responses are indicative of the member's relation to his society and, in addition,

[15] The figures quoted do not add up to 100 since respondents often gave more than one reason.

provide an idea of the importance that the dividend plays at present in that relation. Surprisingly enough, a large majority of *both* activists and ordinary members said they would continue to shop at the Co-op even if it gave no dividend. The proportions were 93 per cent. and 84 per cent., respectively. Two per cent. of the activists and 8 per cent. of the ordinary members replied that they would not continue, the remainder, 5 per cent. and 8 per cent. respectively, answering that they "didn't know". The activists tended to stress ideological reasons for joining the Society and the ordinary members usually offered reasons connected with quality of goods, service and convenience of shops. A small proportion (3 per cent.) of the ordinary members thought the dividend (1s. in the £) too small to matter. Although the replies to this question must be interpreted cautiously, they do suggest that the dividend is not the all-important factor in *retaining* Co-operative loyalty that it is often assumed to be. Quality of goods and service, together with the convenient location of shops, seems to be more important to the ordinary member. From the response to the previous question, it appears, however, that the dividend may be an important factor in *attracting* people to the Co-op in the first place.

In general, the responses to the questions designed to probe the nature of the member's relation to his Society suggests that the division between the apathetic, uninterested majority and the active, interested minority is broadly the same as the division between those who see the Co-op as just another shop (albeit one that gives a dividend) and those who see the Co-op as an expression and part of a wider social movement. The activist's relation is essentially an ideological one: he has a sense of commitment to various ideals, and the Co-op is seen as an instrument for achieving these ideals. Significantly enough, the few activists who said that they would not trade with the Co-op if it gave no dividend justified this attitude on the ground that the dividend was an integral part of the Co-operative ideal, not on the ground of material interest. In contrast, the relation of the ordinary member is essentially that of a customer. He is technically a member of his Society but he is in no sense a member of the Movement. He has no conception of the Co-op except as the place where he is in the habit of trading or as a shop which is conveniently placed. His attitude is markedly unenthusiastic and negative: the Co-op is "as good as" or "no worse than" any other shop. Significantly, the kind of comment he makes when explaining why he joined the Co-op is that one can purchase non-Co-op branded goods there and still get the dividend. And if there were no dividend, he would probably still shop there through habit or because it was convenient to do so.

A series of questions was asked to determine the extent of member participation and knowledge of Co-operation. Ninety-seven per cent. of the sample of ordinary members stated that they did not take part in any activity apart from shopping. None of them had attended the last business meeting held before the inquiry. Moreover, 24 per cent. appeared to be ignorant of the fact that business meetings of members were held and that there were elections of the Board of Directors in which they could vote. However, 7 per cent. claimed to have voted in the election of the Board held a few weeks previously, most of these being members with employee connections. Nine per cent. claimed to have attended a business meeting at some time or other and 15 per cent. to have voted in one of the Society elections. Members who had never attended were asked for their reasons. One in two mentioned lack of time, 32 per cent. stated that they lacked interest or "never went to such things", and 19 per cent. excused themselves on the ground that they lacked knowledge. A further 13 per cent. mentioned age as a reason and 6 per cent. illness. The great bulk of the ordinary members (91 per cent.) could not name a single director of their own society. A similar proportion (89 per cent.) also confessed that they did not know who were the Rochdale Pioneers! (One ventured the guess that they were gold miners!)

The ignorance of the elementary principles of Co-operative organization shown by a significant proportion of the Society's membership may be partly explained by their lack of exposure to the means of communication used in the Society. All new members receive on joining the Society a handbook explaining its organization and activities, but clearly this makes relatively little impact. Posters advertising meetings and elections are placed in the Society's shops, but the non-activists use the shops less frequently than the activists. One in five of the ordinary members stated that they used TASCOS shops less than once a fortnight, compared with one in twenty-five activists in the same category. Another medium of communication between the Society and the members is the *Home Magazine* which contains news about the Society's activities and is distributed gratis in the shops. All but 7.5 per cent. of the activists took this *Magazine,* but 60 per cent. of the ordinary members did not.

As might be expected, the activists in TASCOS are those who trade most with the Society. The respondents were asked to estimate how much per week on the average their family spent at the Co-op. One-third of the ordinary members estimated that they spent less than £1 per week compared with one-tenth of the activists in the same category. At the other end of the scale, one-quarter of the activists claimed to spend over £4 per week compared with one-tenth of the ordinary members.

How active are the activists? A member may be active in various ways. Not all of the activists in TASCOS attend business meetings. Twenty-nine per cent. of our sample, in fact, had not attended any of the last eight quarterly meetings. On the other hand, 55 per cent. claimed to have attended all eight meetings. Three out of four also stated that they had voted in the recently held Board elections. For the majority of activists, however, activity implied more than attending and voting. All but 6 per cent. held or had held offices in the Society and Co-operative Movement, ranging from membership of the Cooperative Wholesale Society Board to membership and office in one of the auxiliary (Guild) organizations. On the average activists held or had held two such offices each.

No attempt was made to determine how knowledgeable were the activists about the Co-operative Movement, but it is clear that the majority were reasonably well-informed. Sixty per cent. stated that they were readers of the national *Co-operative News* and 75 per cent. had heard of the Independent Commission's Report. Many of these respondents were prepared to comment on the Report, most of them favourably.

To be an active participant in an association like a Co-operative involves making a decision as to how one shall use one's leisure time. Since there are numerous voluntary associations, all competing for the limited leisure time of their members, it is conceivable that those who are not active in their Co-operative are active elsewhere. To determine whether this was so, respondents were asked: "What sort of things do you and your husband (or wife) do with your spare time?" The answers to this question do not support the view that the ordinary inactive member is too busily engaged in other associations to have any time to devote to Co-operative affairs. Apart from sport and entertainment such as visiting the cinema, the activities mentioned by respondents could be classified into two main categories: those centred on the home, such as gardening, reading and watching television, and those centred on groups outside the home, such as working for political parties, churches and clubs. There was a marked difference between the responses of the activists and ordinary members. Broadly, the activists tended to mention outside group activities while the ordinary member mentioned activities centred on the home. Thus, while 54 per cent. of the activists were engaged in group activities, only 12 per cent. of the ordinary members were so engaged. On the other hand, 81 per cent. of the ordinary members mentioned home activities, compared with 47 per cent. of the activists. Among the activists there is also to be found the type who may be called the pure Co-operative enthusiast. Six per cent. of the activists stated that *all* their spare-time activity was exclusively connected with their Society.

The distinction among respondents between those who are "group oriented" and those who are "home oriented" is further manifested in activity in trade unions and political parties. The activists (or their husbands or wives) were more likely than others to belong to a trade union and to hold or to have held office in the union. Sixty-three per cent. of the activists or their spouses were trade union members compared with 54 per cent. of the ordinary members. This difference is greater at the level of office-holding. Twenty-one per cent. of the activists held trade union office, at the time of the inquiry, whereas no ordinary member did so. A further 20 per cent. of the activists had formerly held trade union office, compared with 13 per cent. of the ordinary members. Similarly, 71 per cent. of the activists were members of a political party and 32 per cent. held office in a party. The comparable figures for the ordinary members were 16 per cent. and 9 per cent., respectively.

In view of the close association between the British Co-operative Movement and the Labour Party it is interesting to compare the political allegiance of our two sample groups. Respondents were asked: "If there were a general election tomorrow, which party would you vote for?" A majority of both groups declared themselves to be Labour or Labour and Co-operative supporters, but the pro-Labour propensity of the activists was more marked. Eighty-seven per cent. of the activists declared that they would vote Labour or Co-operative and a further 2 per cent. favoured the Communists. Only 53 per cent. of the ordinary members, however, declared themselves to be Labour or Co-operative supporters. Eighteen per cent. were Conservatives and a further 16 per cent. Liberals, the remaining 13 per cent. being classified as "Don't knows". The comparable figures for the activists were 1 per cent. Conservative, 2 per cent. Liberal, 1 per cent. abstentionists. In short, 96 per cent. of the activists compared with 61 per cent. of the ordinary members would have voted for left-wing parties.

This left-wing propensity of the activists is reflected in their newspaper reading habits. The Labour *Daily Herald* was read by 41 per cent. of the activists compared with 12 per cent. of the ordinary members. A more marked contrast was found so far as the Co-operatively-owned Sunday newspaper, *Reynolds News* (now the *Sunday Citizen*) is concerned. Sixty-eight per cent. of the activists were readers of this paper, compared with 4 per cent of the ordinary members.

To complete our picture of the TASCOS activists, several questions were asked concerning the age, sex, marital and occupational statuses of the respondents. On marital status there was no difference between the activists and the general membership. Three out of four in both groups were married, one in five were widowed and the remainder were single. The activists, however, tended to be older than the ordinary members. Only 21 per cent. were under forty-five years of age compared with 29 per cent. of the ordinary members. Perhaps as a consequence of this age difference, the activists tended to be those with a longer record of membership in the Society. All but 2.5 per cent. of them had been members for over ten years, whereas 23 per cent. of the ordinary members had been members for less than ten years. The popular picture of the Co-operative member as "the Woman with the Basket" is supported by the sex distribution figures. Ninety-two per cent. of the ordinary members and 77 per cent. of the activists were women. Of the eighteen male activists in the sample, eleven were employees of the Society. The greater proportion of men among the activists is largely attributable to this employee connection, since, ignoring this group, the proportions of males in the two groups are roughly equal.

Table 7, based on the Registrar-General's classification, gives the occupational status of the two groups, housewives being classified according to their husbands' occupations.

The table shows clearly the working-class character of the So-

Table 7. Occupational Status of Active and Ordinary Members of TASCOS

|  | ACTIVE MEMBERS | ORDINARY MEMBERS |
|---|---|---|
|  | % | % |
| 1. Professional | 1.3 | — |
| 2. Intermediate | 18.9 | 13.5 |
| 3. Skilled | 63.8 | 58.1 |
| 4. Partly skilled | 13.4 | 17.6 |
| 5. Unskilled | 2.6 | 10.8 |
|  | (N = 79) | (N = 74) |

ciety, the majority of members of both groups being either skilled workers or married to skilled workers. The most significant feature of the table however, is the higher occupational status of the activists. Grades 1 and 2 may be considered white-collar middle class occupations. On this basis, 20.2 per cent. of the activists are middle class, compared with 13.5 per cent. of the ordinary members. This difference is in line with the generalization that leadership in voluntary associations, including Co-operatives, is recruited disproportionately from those with high occupational status.

Finally, in an effort to probe the views of the activists on the apathy problem, the question was asked "Why do you think so few members take an interest in their Co-ops?" The answers received to this very general question were, of course, varied. Only one respondent thought there was very little apathy in TASCOS. A few made specific criticisms of the Society's arrangements for democratic control, for example, that the business meetings were not as well advertised as they might be and were held at a place too far away from members living in the outlying districts. Criticisms of those responsible for managing the affairs of the Society were also limited, although one volunteered the view that those who did take an interest were "disgusted at the patronage and nepotism of the system" and another thought that the controlling group had "no ethical ideals" and wanted control in the interests of the Labour Party. Rather more were very conscious that the Society was not attracting younger members and felt that the predominance of the elderly in the Movement discouraged young people from participating. The most frequent explanation of apathy was that the Co-ops suffered from competition of other interests and entertainments, such as television. Others pointed out that nowadays many women are employed outside the home and this, with their domestic commitments, leaves them no time for Co-op activities. Others, again, thought that most members were only interested in the dividend. It was also pointed out by several respondents that apathy was not unique to the Co-operative Movement; it affected other organizations such as trade unions and local government.

The most interesting and significant feature of the replies to this question and general comments made during the interviews, however, was the pessimistic attitude expressed by a substantial minority of activists. This pessimism expresses itself in the form of what appears to be a nostalgia for a "Golden Age" of Co-operation when the organization met the urgent needs of the working-classes and, as a consequence, evoked high enthusiasm. In this attitude two main and connected elements may be discerned. One is the notion that, with the changing social conditions which have improved the status of the workers, there is less need nowadays than formerly for the functions performed by the Co-ops. It was suggested, for example, that the educational and social facilities provided by the Co-ops were becoming redundant now that educational opportunities provided by the State have increased and the workers have money with which to pursue amusements which appeal to them. The higher general standard of living in the post-war years of full employment had had the effect of reducing the worker's need of the Co-op and hence his interest in it as a movement for social reform and amelioration. The other main element in this attitude is the notion that "the old spirit of Co-operation has gone". In part this was seen as a consequence of the diminished zeal for social reform generally and in part as a consequence of the Movement's very success as a trading organization. The increased scale of operation it was felt had resulted in a loss of the personal touch: the elected officials were scattered in the community and were unknown to most members; and the principles of Co-operation had been submerged under the weight of administrative problems. For a few of the more elderly activists this attitude was expressed in the form of an invidious comparison between the generations. The old-style Co-operators imbued with zeal and principles were passing away and being replaced by new people who had no real understanding of Co-operative ideals. To such activists the present generation appeared ungrateful and unappreciative of what the old-timers had done; and they had a deep-seated suspicion that, as they themselves died off, there would be no-one left worthy to carry the torch of Co-operation.

It is no part of our present purpose to discuss what validity there is in this attitude. It must suffice to point out that it is symptomatic of a malaise which, if it continues to spread, threatens the very heart of Co-operative democracy.

In summary, then, the profile of the activist compared with the ordinary member is that he is more likely to have come from a Co-operative family and to have a wife or husband who is also a member. He or, rather, she (since the typical activist is a woman) is older, has a longer record of membership, and enjoys a higher occupational status. She frequents the Society and shops more often and spends more than the ordinary member. Her spare-time activities are centered on outside groups rather than on the home. She, or her husband, is a trade unionist, often an active one. Politically, the activist is more strongly pro-Labour and Co-operative and is more likely to be both a member and an officer in a political party. Her left-wing political outlook is reflected in the newspapers she takes and she is more likely to be linked with the Co-operative network of communication through reading Co-operative journals and papers. She is more likely than the ordinary member to have an employee connection with the Society, either through her husband or through a relative, especially a connection at the managerial level. At the same time, her attachment to the Society is primarily ideological. The ordinary member sees the Co-op essentially as a shop and has no knowledge of or interest in the ideological side and no intention of joining in any Co-operative activity. The ordinary member is a customer for whom it might be said the question of opting out of participation has never arisen; she has never thought of herself as "in" the Society at all. In marked contrast the activist is more than a customer: she is deeply involved in the Society and sees herself as the member of a social movement. For her Co-operation may be a movement which has lost some of its old ideals, but it remains a movement and not merely a business.

## Suggestions for Further Reading

JEAN BLONDEL, *Voters, Parties and Leaders* (Harmondsworth: Penguin Books, 1963). Subtitled "The Social Fabric of British Politics," the aim of this book was to examine the studies made at all levels of British society in order to draw some general conclusions about the workings of the political system. It is an outstanding reference book.

THOMAS BOTTOMORE, "Social Stratification in Voluntary Organisations," in David V. Glass, ed., *Social Mobility in Britain* (London: Routledge and Kegan Paul, 1954). This study has two parts. (1) In the English county town of Hertford, 135 voluntary organizations were identified and some general information obtained from them about the occupations of the membership and of the leadership. Although this is not identical with the division between nonactivists and activists in *Power in Co-operatives,* it is close enough for useful comparisons. (2) Four organizations were studied in greater detail, including the personal friendships of the members.

JOSEPH GOLDSTEIN, *The Government of British Trade Unions* (London: Allen and Unwin, 1952). Although the title of this book is misleading since it is the report of a study of a single British trade union, the Transport and General Workers' Union, the text makes a useful comparison with *Power in Co-operatives* because it examines the constitution and voting practices of another democratic organization. Goldstein also reports on the activities of a single branch of the union which he joined in order to participate in the democratic process.

W. L. GUTTSMAN, *The British Political Elite* (London: MacGibbon and Kee, 1963). This volume is an excellent historical and statistical account of Members of Parliament and other political leaders since 1868. Chapters 11 and 12 widen its coverage to consider the political elite against the wider background of a power elite and the concept of democracy in British society.

ROBERT MC KENZIE, *British Polical Parties,* 2d ed. (London: Heinemann, 1963). A classic study of the iron law of oligarchy in terms of the distribution of power within the Conservative and Labour parties, it concludes that the realities of eighty years of party organization in Britain do not confirm Michels' pessimistic thesis.

# ᏔᏅ Pentonville

## TERENCE AND PAULINE MORRIS

*All societies make some provision for dealing with what they regard as serious delinquents. In England at the end of the eighteenth and the beginning of the nineteenth centuries, capital punishment for a large number of crimes was largely replaced by transportation overseas to some part of the rapidly growing empire. Eventually this method of disposing of the criminal gave way to the institution of long-term imprisonment. At the present time there are three central maximum-security prisons in England for men—Dartmoor, Parkhurst, and Pentonville. There are also a number of local prisons and four regional prisons, like the one at Maidstone, which attempt to rehabilitate the prisoner into society at the end of his sentence by providing training in occupational skills while he is serving his time. Delinquent boys, between the ages of sixteen and twenty-one, are put to Borstal or one of the other "open" training prisons modeled after it.*

*A prisoner is not normally sent to Pentonville unless he has previously served a prison sentence. Thus, the community described in the following selection consists of individuals who, when they are not in prison, make a living largely through crime and near-criminal*

SOURCE: Terence and Pauline Morris, assisted by Barbara Barer, *Pentonville: A Sociological Study of an English Prison*, Chapters 10 and 11 (pp. 214–49). Copyright © 1963 by Terence Morris and Pauline Morris. Reprinted by permission of Routledge & Kegan Paul Ltd and Humanities Press Inc.

*activities; and they are kept in order by men who have spent most of their working lives serving in Pentonville or prisons like it.*

*Mr. and Mrs. Morris spent fifteen months in Pentonville where they were allocated an office as the base from which to conduct their work. Their aim was to describe and analyze the nature of social relationships in a restricted community. Staff members and prisoners alike were invited to visit them in the research office whenever the opportunity presented itself and they felt so inclined, and the researchers were permitted to wander freely about the prison, observing what went on and talking to prisoners and prison staff members. Much of the data, indeed, was obtained from informal conversations carried out in this way; however, formal interviews were carried out with about one third of the staff. Each prisoner completed a "census" form on his age, marital status, birthplace, age of leaving school, etc., and prison records were also analyzed. The researchers attended the morning conferences of the warden (or governor) with the guards, as well as other prison meetings as and when they occurred. Some prisoners wrote essays, selections from which were reproduced as an appendix to the book. As the authors themselves put it, much of their knowledge of prison life came not so much from this kind of data but from simply "being on the premises," and they recorded a daily diary which ran by the end of the study to 700,000 words, which were indexed, classified, and analyzed by Mrs. Barbara Barer.*

Pentonville *is very much preoccupied with a description and analysis of the social structure of an isolated community organized around the notion of punishment. Although the authors are aware of public discussions about the function of prisons as reformatories where delinquents may be treated and trained to cope with the realities of normal life, what impressed them most about their fifteen months in Pentonville was that containment and control were the dominant objectives. Even the architectural appearance of their surroundings emphasized this conclusion to them. This does not mean that they paid no attention to the welfare provisions attempted in the prison, but they saw them as overshadowed by the pressing daily demands of feeding, clothing, and housing a large body of men and*

*keeping them out of mischief. The analysis of cooperation and con-
flict among staff and prisoners must be read against the background
of such imperatives.*

*Research in any organization runs up against problems arising
from the acceptance or rejection of the idea of research itself and of
the personalities of the researchers. Research in prisons is further
complicated by the very special nature of the significance of incarceration for most of the inmates. In this case Mr. and Mrs. Morris
had to face the fact that never in the history of Pentonville had a
woman been given free range to walk around unescorted on the
premises. From some of the prison staff they also had to face a certain amount of hostility which increased a little over time, although
throughout the inquiry staff hostility was neither uniform nor widespread. Prisoners, on the other hand, became more cooperative. From
this point of view* Pentonville *is an outstanding example of what
can be achieved through patient perserverance and tact.*

## Communication and Conflict among the Staff

The staff of Pentonville, especially the uniformed staff, are
frequently at loggerheads with each other. The reasons for this internal conflict are partly structural, that is to say, they originate in the
organization of the work situation itself. In this respect they differ
hardly at all with the dissensions which characterize almost every
collective work situation, whether it be a university department, an
insurance office, a factory or a building site. In part, however, they
stem from a clash of personalities which occurs in the process of
mutual evaluation. In Pentonville there are wide ideological differences and varying perceptions of the functions of imprisonment.
There are, for example, opponents as well as supporters of capital
and corporal punishment. In addition, there are economic jealousies
and, most fundamental of all, problems which stem from the fact
that some people simply do not like each other.

Some officers felt that backbiting at Pentonville was excessive.
As one man put it, 'Cattiness was bad enough in the [armed] forces,

but here it's worse. All [that the] men are worried about is overtime and pay rises. You can't keep a thing to yourself.' Another, nostalgically recalling from his service life what he called 'esprit de corps', said, 'Here they do nothing but backbite.'

Certain officers were always causing difficulties for their colleagues, and in a closed community such as Pentonville the opportunities for internecine feuds to develop are legion. The backbiting and gossip which exists among the staff outside working hours is paralleled in the work situation. These tensions and conflicts tend to be aggravated by the negative aspects of authoritarianism which flourish like bacteria in an environment which tends to be organizationally confused.

The structural element in the internal conflicts of the Pentonville staff derives very largely from the shortcomings of the actual administration and organization of duties. . . . Personality tends, however, to creep in. Officers also tended to criticize each other for 'convenience' sickness.

There is little doubt that the considerable amount of shouting that takes place in Pentonville does little to enhance the dignity and authority of the staff, especially when officers are shouting at each other. Other forms of hostility do not go wholly unnoticed. Thus a prisoner in H Wing said that he did not think it right that quarrels between the staff should be played out in front of prisoners, they should keep them private. That morning an officer in H Wing had not got his breakfast until 9.10 a.m. because his relief officer had not come back at the proper time; this resulted in some recrimination.

Behaviour of this kind was merely at one end of a whole spectrum of behaviour which one P[rison] O[fficer] described as childish, and typical of many of the younger officers. At the other end were instances of horseplay and practical joking. It is likely, however, that joking relationships, although undignified on occasion, do less damage on the whole to the officers' prestige in prisoners' eyes than the open hostility at the other end of the scale.

One of the characteristics of the Pentonville staff which was observed was its collective inertia. In one officer's words, many were 'just like sheep'. Nowhere was this more apparent than in the officers' mess. During the research period the officers' dining-room became increasingly crowded, while the adjacent card room remained comparatively empty. Then, day by day, officers gradually filtered into the card room to eat, until within a few weeks the situation was completely reversed. Furthermore, the food they ate was of such an appalling quality that if it were served to prisoners a major riot might well have ensued. Although individually they constantly grumbled, they took no effective action either as individuals or collectively

The reasons for this inertia are likely to be found in the general atmosphere of Pentonville in which subordinate officers are most reluctant to express criticism to their superiors, or indeed to question affairs for fear that to do so will have bad repercussions upon them and their chances of promotion; as one said, 'You would be a fool to argue the toss, especially while on probation'. Subordinate officers see their superiors either as excessively rigid or alternatively so frightened of their own shadows that they avoid any decision or action which might be controversial, and observation tended to confirm this view. At the same time, many officers were afraid to use initiative, because as one put it: 'If you ask a senior officer, you are asked why the hell you bother him, and if you don't, and something goes wrong, you are asked why the hell you didn't.'

Timidity, inertia and anxiety about promotion and official reports colour, too, another dimension of staff relations, namely, those between older and younger officers. It is a commonplace in Pentonville that any new idea which may have been implanted on a training or refresher course is soon discarded, for the pressure of peers is too great to be resisted.

It is virtually axiomatic in Pentonville that a prisoner should not be given reasons for what is done or not done. The discipline officer, too, shares to some extent the same frustrations which stem from being ill-informed. Because the concept of rationality is inherent in the structure of bureaucracy the 'ideal' officer has no anxiety about the wisdom or practicability of decisions which are communicated to him. Still less should he question statements of policy which come from the Governor's Office. In practice, the contingent decisions which are at the heart of the day-to-day running of the prison require all staff members, in varying degrees, to act flexibly. This they can seldom do if they are not in possession of *reasons* as well as instructions.

At the most senior level the Governor's morning conference permits a mutual feed-back of information between the Governor, the Deputy Governor and the Chaplain. The Steward and the Chief Officer are present whenever business concerning them is being discussed. Instructions to the staff are communicated verbally by the Chief to the assembled officers on the Centre. In brief, it can be said that information flows downwards in the hierarchy, but explanations tend to be filtered out at each level. Communication, like water, flows in an upward direction only with difficulty. The discipline officer can make verbal approaches to all his uniformed superiors, but above this level normally needs to 'put in a paper' to the Governor.

In quite small matters increased information would make for greater efficiency. On one occasion an officer was unlocking prisoners for a lecture. The senior officer did not know what the lecture was about, so that he could not tell the junior officers, and they in turn were unable to tell the prisoners. Delay and indecision resulted whilst men made up their minds whether to attend and hope they would not be bored, or risk missing something really interesting. More importantly, such deprivation of elementary information tends to reduce the status of the officer to an automatic turnkey-cum-sheepdog.

Failure of communication and lack of information, especially about Commissioners' policy, was mentioned on occasions too frequent to cite. Many of the complaints were about the lack of orders in writing. The desire to have things in writing is consistent with the inability to tolerate ambiguity and the general inertia which has already been discussed. As one officer, who had recently left a fixed post on the gate, put it, 'They ask you why you don't use your initiative, but when you do, it is wrong'.

Because prisoners are not inhibited as officers are, in the matter of by-passing the formal bureaucratic procedures, the myth that 'the prisoners run the prison' is reinforced. One officer discussed the difficulty of getting anything done through official channels. A few days before he had wanted a piece of hardboard for the Wing Office, had acquired a chit from the Foreman of Works, and had duly presented it at the Stores, only to be told that he could not have any. He mentioned this to his red-band * who said, 'Leave it to me, Sir', and came back in an hour or so with the hardboard. The significance of this incident is that it becomes part of the structure of staff beliefs about the administration of the prison. Because the process of remembering is highly selective, a set of expectations about 'official behaviour' develops in which inefficiency and illogicality are norms of expectation.

The Consultative Committee in Pentonville, set up by order of the Commissioners, represents in theory a considerable modification to the hierarchical authority structure of the prison. It meets quarterly and consists of the Governor, Deputy Governor, Chief Officer, Medical Officer, Foreman of Works, six officers representing different sections of the prison and a member of the civilian staff as Secretary. Topics ranged from those originating from Head Office memoranda to those initiated by members of the Committee. Records of the proceedings of the Committee indicated that discussion led to certain minor actions—for example, the erection of notice boards on the exercise yards—but that other subjects, such as the issue of socks and shirts to prisoners, frequently recurred as topics for discussion. Indeed, one officer resigned from the Committee because, he said, 'all they discuss is shirts.' Although comparatively trivial in themselves, the cumulative effect of such minor issues in the prison is considerable, and the minutes of the Committee reveal that discussion was frequently constructive although practical results were not necessarily forthcoming.

Attempts to discuss prison problems constructively could occasionally backfire. Thus at one meeting an officer made a number of

* A red-band is a prisoner assigned a position of trust by the officers. He is allowed to move freely about the prison.—Ed.

positive suggestions about improving the details of Reception procedure. The result of this was that the Chief Officer immediately went down to Reception and implied to the Reception P[rison] O[fficer] that he gathered the job was not being done properly, and therefore he should 'hold everything' as an inquiry would be made. When the officer reported on the meeting of the Consultative Committee to the Reception P.O. he met with considerable hostility.

The shortcomings of the Consultative Committee were nevertheless apparent. In the first place the rank and file of the staff felt it to be remote. Delegacy is in fact an inadequate substitute for participation, and the size of the Committee effectively precluded any genuine feeling that the junior staff *as a whole* had been given a share in the discussion and formulation of policy. Secondly, the senior staff tended to overbalance the Committee, and officers were by and large reluctant to participate on a basis of equality with those who in all other structural contexts had to be treated with the deference due to superiors. Thirdly, the functions of the Committee tended to overlap with the meetings of the Governor and Chief with the representatives of the P[rison] O[fficers'] A[ssociation] Branch, creating a certain degree of confusion in the minds of those staff members who were remote from either the Consultative Committee or the branch organization. The sheer size of Pentonville raises problems in this field of communication which would appear to require some modification of the existing Consultative Committee arrangements.

## Co-operation and Conflict among the Captives

. . . . .

The prisoner in Pentonville has, almost without exception, undergone incarceration before. He may have been in approved schools from an early age, spent his adolescence in Borstal and his young manhood in prison, with the result that normal socialization and prisonization have been merged imperceptibly in a common spectrum of experience. Even in a recidivist prison like Pentonville, therefore, differential exposure to the process of prisonization is an important factor in contributing to the heterogeneous character of the population. Some men will still react to social stimuli in ways which would be appropriate in the world outside, while others will behave in a completely prisonized fashion and have few reference points for their actions other than those which exist exclusively within the prison community.

Save those whose adjustment to the experience of imprisonment takes the form of social or psychological withdrawal—those who choose either to be solitaries or to indulge in the narcotic of "reverie-plus'—all prisoners must participate in the activities of the prison community. Privacy is rare and the prison day, for all its monotonous boredom, is a long one. Superficially, the prison has the qualities of mass society, the uniformity of basic values, standardization in consumption patterns, and power which is concentrated in a bureaucratic organization beyond the scope of influence by the individual. The routine behaviour of the staff appears to be no less standardized than the reactions of the prisoners. In fact, on closer examination, the monolithic images of staff and prisoners are far from uniform. Because a common normative thread of attitudes and behaviour runs through the activities of each, the general effect from a distance is one of uniformity, whereas in reality, both staff and prisoner groups are like impressionist paintings in which dots of many different colours combine to produce a general effect. We have already attempted to examine the dynamic aspects of intra-staff relationships; we now turn to those who are the helots of the prison community.

In theory the organizational structure of the prison does not recognize the existence of individual relationships among prisoners except in negative terms. This is a legacy of the nineteenth century when the prevention of contamination, in the sphere of morals no less than physical health, demanded rigid segregation—individual cells, hoods on exercise, separate stalls in chapel and treadmill house, and above all, silence. Communication between prisoners was regarded as synonymous with conspiracy to plan mischief, either in the prison or in the shape of future crime outside. In consequence, even after the hoods and the chapel partitions had long disappeared, restrictions on inter-prisoner communication remained. It was not until the final abolition of the silence rule on exercise in the 1940s, and in the workshops in the mid-1950s, that social intercourse for the Pentonville prisoner became relatively free. Even at the time of writing (1961) 'association' periods are limited to the men in H Wing and to fewer than 100 selected long-termers in the main prison. Furthermore, men may not lawfully enter each other's cells.

Thus, over the years in Pentonville there has grown up a pattern of covert communication—a secret language of signs and gestures, systems of message-carrying and ingenious devices for the passing of illicit notes. Writers, as separated in time as McCartney (1936) and Norman (1958), both discuss the ingenious technology whereby prisoners circumvent the restrictions on communication and, Prometheus-like, re-learn the secret of making fire.[1] The inertia which is a characteristic of all value systems is no less marked in the culture of the prison community, and institutional procedures which were developed in response to the unambiguous repression of former years persist among the prisoners of Pentonville. Heirs to more than a century of prison culture, they cannot, even if they were willing, wholly disinherit themselves.

If Pentonville is no longer, to borrow Bentham's phrase, 'a mill for grinding rogues honest and idle men industrious', it will seek to impose a common experience upon its inmates. Whether the intention is to train, or merely to contain, is immaterial; what is important is that the activities of the prison authorities impose sufficiently well-defined social constraints as to enable prisoners to experience a sense of social solidarity and collective identity. Stripped of their material possessions and largely deprived of individual freedom, every prisoner is, in one sense, a member of a community of social paupers. Thus

[1] Fire-making, in the days when smoking was forbidden, was a developed art. But the tinder box—still carried by 'old timers' from Dartmoor and Parkhurst—is, like its American counterpart the glim wheel, fast disappearing from Pentonville. In prisons like Maidstone and the Scrubs it is said by prisoners to have disappeared altogether.

the very social forces which strip the individual prisoner bare to facilitate the task of his containment, at the same time create a sense of identity among the faceless mass. Prisoners cannot escape living together and it becomes imperative that inter-prisoner conflict be reduced to a minimum; the external pressures of the prison create problems enough without the additional burden of internecine struggles. But the deprivations of imprisonment stimulate prisoners to go further than this; they represent a challenge which is answered by a whole variety of ingenious social and technological devices designed to reduce deprivation to a minimum. To buttress these routinized procedures a system of social control has emerged. It differs hardly at all from the 'hoodlum code' described by Leopold for the Illinois Penitentiary at Statesville-Joliet,[2] from the accounts of Clemmer [3] and Sykes,[4] or from those reported by McCartney [5] and Norman.[6] The 'con' learns to do his bird, he does not 'rat', 'grass', 'shop' or inform; he takes every opportunity to exploit the prison to his own advantage and he co-operates with his captors only to the extent which is necessary to prevent 'the heat' being turned on himself and his fellows.

In practice things do not work so smoothly. The prison contains men who are intellectually unable to perceive that co-operation serves their interest better than uncoordinated individualism. Some, by reason of mental defect or mental disorder, are incapable of sustained rational behaviour in any event. Some have personalities so psychopathic that for greed and their own selfish advantage they consistently exploit their fellows. Some belong to groups which are socially marginal or of pariah status in the outside world—coloured men and sex offenders. Behaviour among prisoners, far from representing a consistently cohesive reaction to the demands of the prison, oscillates about an uneasy internal equilibrium.

Observations in both Pentonville and Maidstone indicate that

[2] Nathan Leopold, *Life + 99 Years,* London, Gollancz, 1958.

[3] Donald Clemmer, *The Prison Community,* Boston, 1940.

[4] Gresham Sykes, *The Society of Captives,* Princeton, 1958.

[5] W. F. McCartney, *Walls Have Mouths,* London, 1936.

[6] Frank Norman, *Bang to Rights,* London, 1958.

the content of inmate sub-culture is explicable in terms of its *prob-lem-solving* qualities (easing the pains of imprisonment), rather than in terms of *negative selection* (all prisoners have crime in common and share opposition to the conventional norms of society). How it arose in the first place is essentially a problem of conjectural history, and is, in our view, scarcely relevant. In considering the pattern of inmate sub-culture we are in substantial agreement with Schrag,[7] and Sykes and Messenger.[8] A proportion of the prisoner population is indeed integrated with a criminal sub-culture outside, and ... such integration has an important effect upon both the persistence of deviant values and upon relationships in the prison. But a number of men are not in fact so integrated and their participation in the inmate sub-culture indicates a functional response to the experience of imprisonment rather than a wholesale commitment to a criminal value system on an abstract level.

## Social Groupings and Patterns of Prisoner Relationships

Relationships are regulated by the constraints imposed by the prison as much as by personal choice. No prisoner can choose his cell, or his cell mates, and although the staff are often prepared to be accommodating to individuals, men are normally thrown together without regard to individual preference. Men in a 'three-cell' together must of necessity attempt to 'get on' with each other or life is in-tolerable, but there is no indication that such enforced intimacy gives rise to lasting associations. The prisoner's life is spent be-tween cell, workshop and exercise yard, and in each of these areas he generally finds the same faces. In the Chapel, and in concerts and lectures, men are distributed by location, and it is only in the sick parade, the hospital, or the queue outside the Governor's Office that a prisoner is likely to see men from parts of the prison other

[7] Clarence Schrag, 'Social Types in a Prison Community', unpublished Master's Thesis, Univ. of Washington, 1944.
[8] Gresham Sykes and Sheldon Messenger, 'The Inmate Social System', in *Theoretical Studies in the Social Organisation of the Prison,* 1960.

than his own. The chances are that a prisoner's friends—or relatives —may be distributed anywhere in the prison.

*Physical immobility* and *problems of communication* are thus important limiting factors in the range of the individual prisoner's social contacts; nevertheless the *intensity* of relationships will vary in terms of other factors. The spectrum of relationships seen by a prisoner resulted in the following perspective:

There are mates, friends, and acquaintances. Mates you do anything for; you give them anything they want and if he is involved in a punch up you go in. Friends you lend to but you don't give. If he's in a punch up you think about what might be involved before you go in. Acquaintances you don't want to know, and you couldn't care less what happens in a punch up. I have 2 mates, about a dozen friends and thousands of acquaintances.

The intensity of relationship is thus determined as much by the scale of the 'mass society of captives' as by choice. Informants invariably gave a sociometric picture which contained one mate, three or four friends, and dozens of acquaintances. The restraints upon social intercourse restrict the range of contact appreciably, but more important, the character of prison life makes it dangerous for a man to be intimate with more than the small handful of men whom he feels he can trust. It is not unknown for a prisoner to become friendly with another and discover the whereabouts of that prisoner's wife or sister, and then, if he is released before his 'friend', ingratiate himself for financial and—occasionally—for sexual gain.

According to one informant, each man has a mate, and 'only mates know what each other is doing.' Mates are chosen preferably on the basis of long acquaintanceship, preferably through previous Borstal and prison sentences, and possibly on the outside as well. Life in the prison community is fraught not only with the frustrations and deprivations imposed by imprisonment itself, but also with the dangers of violence, intimidation, and exploitation by other inmates. The relationships between mates therefore are both defensive alliances as well as reciprocal supports against the deprivations of imprisonment. Men often read their mate's letters, and sometimes ask a

Prison Visitor if he could visit the mate as well. Between mates there can be no grassing; indeed, between friends it is frowned upon. A man in a position to discover the intentions of the staff is morally obliged to pass on such intelligence for the benefit of his friends and mates, though by no means for the benefit of others.

The pattern of selection depends upon various criteria. Mates and friends must belong to the inmate's 'own class'. There must be a cultural and ideological identity in order to achieve the equality which is an essential element in such relationships.

Some find a common bond by mixing with people from their home town. Others tend to look for friends who have proved themselves on previous sentences. Some look for those with similar sentences to their own, thus ensuring that they have pals for all their stay in prison. Some, like myself, just drift from one to another.

This extract is from an essay by a prisoner of superior intelligence and education who, like many of his kind, tended to be a social isolate. Another prisoner in an essay wrote:

A cultured person on entering prison finds he is quite up against it, for instance he has to mix with people who absolutely go against his own ways and manners therefore he is being punished quite hard by having to try and adapt himself to other people's ways, ways that are not very nice, but what is nice in prison? What is culture in here?, it's like watching a beautiful red Rose die. . . .

Apart from such social differences which would separate men in the outside world there are other factors making for social stratification among the prisoner population which are meaningful only in the context of the institution. One of these is a combination of age and prison experience. Throughout the research a comparatively small number of men from Dartmoor and Parkhurst were in the prison, either for purposes of accumulated visits or legal proceedings in the High Court. Dartmoor and Parkhurst men do not mix more than they are obliged to with Pentonville 'natives', even those who are serving relatively long sentences of three years or more. Research observations and the statements of Dartmoor and Parkhurst informants are in substantial agreement on this point. The pay of these 'visitors' is considerably higher (being on a different rate and increased by stage money). Their reference group remains very firmly their 'own' prison, which some of the older men still refer to as their 'penal station'.[9]

Among Pentonville's 'natives' there is a similar trend towards the formation of an élite, generally among men whose criminal careers are similar to those of the Dartmoor/Parkhurst group, but who are currently serving short sentences rather than long ones. Among them persists what is known as the 'Old Pals' Act.

The Old Pals' Act may be likened to a kind of crude freemasonry among men who believe themselves to be, within the prison community, a limited and socially superior élite. The grouping which this élite implies is essentially diffuse and may be likened to the totemic ties which loosely bind distant relatives in certain primitive societies. It is in no way a substitute for those groupings which arise in the form of cliques or gangs, and which are the principal groupings for action in the prisoner community. Rather, the Old Pals' Act tends to make for a special reciprocity in 'mate' relationships. One of its dominant characteristics is that goods and services which are normally obtained by illicit economic exchanges are the subject of genuine 'giving' among 'Old Pals'. Although altruism and reciprocity in this sense exist between Old Pals, the Old Pals' Act is more of an abstract psychological concept rather than a collective reality. In many ways it bears some resemblance to the diffuse identity of interest which links so-called 'members' of the *Mafia*. While there is comparatively uniform hostility to other out groups, there is no guarantee against factionalism from within. Indeed, the alignment of social forces within the prison is generally such as to make the Old Pals' Act a relatively unimportant factor in the distribution of power and influence.

In addition to age, criminal experience, institutional record, and social background, there are other variables which contribute to the stratification of the prisoner group.

[9] A term which is at least 100 years old.

*Offence* tends by and large to be a negative criterion, that is to say certain types of offence tend to degrade a man's status in the eyes of his fellow inmates whereas few offences carry an automatic bonus of prestige. Thus while a particularly daring robbery, or a very large haul, may well enhance a man's reputation, it will do so to a much smaller degree than will, say, a sex offence operate to *reduce* his status. Criminal competence has some bearing upon status, but as prisoners consistently distort and exaggerate the extent of their crimes when they happen to have been of the status producing variety, this particular currency is, as it were, permanently devalued as it is known to be consistently debased. Now that the author of the wages snatch with his Commando-like precision seriously challenges the traditional status of such craftsmen in crime as the safe-breaker,[10] there is a genuine difference of opinion, at least among those whose social orientations are primarily criminal, as to who is the aristocrat of the prison world. Housebreaking and larceny are lower in the hierarchy—'anyone can do a Yale with a bit of celluloid' —but more prestigeful than 'paper crimes' like forgery. Crimes against the person, and property crimes involving considerable violence are not, however, the subject of value consensus. Violence on the whole tends to be relatively acceptable to men in the 20—25 age group, but is rather less acceptable to men of 35 and over. This is due partly to generational differences in outlook, and partly to the role which physical violence plays in the social system of the prison. The problem of the sex offenders is a complex one, for . . . certain offences like rape and carnal knowledge carry little stigma if the woman or girl concerned could be regarded as a desirable (if illicit) sexual object by a 'normal' man. Where children are concerned, prisoners are excessively sentimental, and in consequence an offender against a *child* as opposed to a sexually precocious or prematurely developed adolescent is ensured pariah status. Such offenders will frequently go to some length to try and conceal their offences, though these are often thwarted, either by other prisoners or by the staff.

[10] The Eastcastle Street Mail Van Robbery, which took place in 1952, is generally regarded by the professionals as one of the 'great jobs' of all time.

Pentonville also contains at any given time a number of vagrants, drunks and similar social derelicts. By and large these are old men, serving very short sentences of a few days or at most a few weeks, often in lieu of a fine. Many of them are unclean in their personal habits, and prison argot classifies them all as *slags,* and those who are or were verminous as *fumes.* Their crimes, apart from begging, wandering abroad or drunkenness, are invariably petty— the theft of a raincoat, a bottle of milk or pennies from a news-stand. The younger prisoners, especially those who may be described as *professional* in the sense that they seek to make a livelihood from crime, regard this particular type of offender as of contemptible status.

Offence, and previous penal institutional experience, are sometimes combined with length of sentence as criteria of status. Thus as far as the *professional* criminal is concerned, Borstal ('*College*'), which for many is no more than an ante-chamber to the prison world, is a mark of some distinction. 'Pentonville natives' who are serving long sentences of four years or more tend to regard themselves as an élite, rather as the Dartmoor and Parkhurst men do, but often have relationships with short-termers who happen to fall within the category of 'Old Pals'. Broadly speaking a *lagging* [11] (3 years) invests the individual with more status than a *stretch* (12 months), and a *carpet* (3 months) more than a *tramp's lagging* [12] (14 days).

The essential point about all these factors making for stratification in the prison community is that they are, irrespective of the verbalizations of informants, relatively diffuse in consequence of the heterogeneity of the inmate population. The individual prisoner has no social chart by which he can navigate in the often treacherous currents of the prison. The population changes, the social barometer fluctuates between tensions and calm and the balance of opposing

[1] These terms are of ancient derivation. One prisoner suggested that 'lagging' was derived from the days when convicts were 'lagged' or fettered, and 'carpet' from the period it took a man to make a carpet or mat on the weaving frame in his cell.

[2] The invidious yet humorous overtones of this phrase reflect with some accuracy the vagrant's low status.

social forces in the inmate group is subject to constant if sometimes imperceptible change. Apart from certain types of sex offenders, the only prisoner who can make predictions about his status in the institution and other prisoners' attitudes towards him is the coloured man.

The number of coloured men in Pentonville at any time is small. At the time of the research census 2.16 per cent of the population were classed as full negro, 0.8 per cent as mixed negro, and 0.56 per cent as Asian. Thus approximately 3.5 per cent of the population was recognizably non-white to both prisoners and staff. A further 0.88 per cent were classified as Levantine (Turks, Cypriots, etc.) in that they were of swarthy appearance which made them markedly distinct from the rest of the population. Collectively, these men constituted a minority which was too small to be ignored, yet insufficiently large to be inconspicuously integrated with the community as a whole.

Attitudes to coloured prisoners followed the pattern which is well established among lower-class urban whites outside; it is primarily xenophobic and one which does not discriminate between West Africans, West Indians, or coloured men born in the U.K. who are lumped together as 'spooks', 'spades', or 'darkies'. Nor is there any evidence to suggest that Indians and Pakistanis are regarded as anything more than a sub-species of 'spook', 'spade' or 'darkie'. The following extracts from an essay by a young prisoner with a record of violence, entitled *Racial Riotes,* illustrate the prevailing pattern of attitudes and beliefs.

I am saying about 10 out or every 100 coloured People work for a living in this country, the rest life off the National assistance U.A.B. and draw money Each week, in addition money from there own government.

. . . spades are forever holding Parties . . . with Big Radio sound system

Cram which Make a terrible nose . . . and when the next morning comes and you want to use the W/C you will find it stacked with beer bottles, uring all over the floor and people complaned of finding French letters and so forth. No attempt is made by these people to clean there Mess up affter them. White Women have to do it.

Drugs are taken by these coloured People. Hemp. Spanish fly, opim and Mariquona. When they have taken these drugs they become abusive and Violent.

With the Money (they make from prostitution) the buy knew cars and they are all new, the best type of cars. Ordinary White man has to work hard all his life and save up to buy a car. They can't draw doll like colored People do.

This chronicler of Notting Hill goes on to accuse the coloured population of attacking women at night, organizing pickpockets in the Portobello Road Market and

. . . making the Royal Bouroth (of Kensington) worse than it already is.

Sexual jealousy, competition for unskilled work, and for housing, the costs of which are forced up as the area becomes increasingly a coloured ghetto, combined with resentment and envy at the flamboyant clothes and the large cars with which coloured men are seen. Inside the prison, the uncomplimentary stereotype of the coloured man is reinforced by the fact that coloured prisoners in Pentonville are in most instances serving sentences for offences associated with prostitution.

Racial discrimination in the prison takes a variety of subtle forms. The research worker noticed that on the door of a small storeroom in the Wood Shed was inscribed in chalk

### 'SMOKING LOUNGE—NO BLACK BASTARD'

In asking about the origins of this inscription a discussion ensued in which a group of prisoners all agreed that 'spades, wogs, and Maltese' were the 'lowest of the low', that they were dirty in their personal habits, were brothel keepers, and always managed to jump the housing queue. One man claimed that he had 'done six months for hitting a black'. His wife had been pregnant, and because the coloured man had, he alleged, pushed her off the pavement, 'I just got the nearest thing in my hand which was a shopping bag with tins in it, and smashed him across the face with it.' On another occasion a group of men in the Mailbag Shop tied the braces of an Indian prisoner to his heavy chair with a piece of twine. This man was a surly individual who normally spoke to no one. As he got up at the end of labour the chair rose with him, and in a fury he swung round to face his tormentors. The chair gyrated with him and caused confusion in the confined space which set everyone laughing. This served to make him even angrier.

It is rare for actual fighting to break out between whites and non-whites, though a pitched battle, three a side, did occur on one occasion. Some coloured men are able to give a good account of themselves, and one in particular during the research period enjoyed respect as a 'tearaway' despite his colour. Most of the coloured population is undoubtedly socially marginal even with reference to the coloured population outside; the position of those who are relatively well educated is therefore particularly acute. As one put it: 'Intelligent people in prison are very often isolated, but an intelligent coloured person is hopelessly isolated. I don't see any answer to this. It's just a question of social evolution.'

Pentonville men possess three qualities in common: (1) being subjected to the rigours of a maximum security prison; (2) having been labelled criminals by the outside world, and (3) (in all but a very few instances) having been in prison before. Only in the most extreme circumstances are these qualities sufficient to produce inmate solidarity by themselves; che degree of integration exhibited by prisoners derives also from the functional interdependence of individuals whose co-operative activities are directed towards the reduction of the pains of imprisonment. The solidarity of the prisoner section of the community is therefore neither wholly organic nor wholly mechanical, but tends to oscillate, depending upon context. Thus at an ideological level 'all cons must stick together', but at the level of immediate reality solidarity depends upon the constellation of individual relationships. It is only in specific situations that the issues are so unambiguously stated that the cohesive values of the inmate social code are clear. The facts of imprisonment and criminality by themselves are insufficient, and the passions associated with quarrels and feuds can run high. As one informant put it: 'Any man who thinks there is honour among thieves should be choked to death when he said it.' The ties that bind prisoners together most effectively are the relationships which develop as individuals and groups enter into contractual relations to lessen the deprivations of imprisonment. This elaborate system of contractual relations is an essential feature of the subculture of the prison, and consists of the whole range of illicit enterprises by which prisoners create goods and services for each other, or achieve a reallocation of those which are provided by the prison authorities.

## The Nature of Illicit Enterprise

The Prison Rules are so comprehensive that any relationship or activity initiated by a prisoner could theoretically constitute an offence. 'Unauthorised articles' are any which are not specifically allocated or permitted by the prison authorities. Any service by one prisoner for another is similarly unlawful. In any community where demand and scarcity coexist there is a stimulus to manufacture and supply; where both demand and scarcity are acute it follows that individuals will be prepared to take considerable risks in order to profit from the situation. These risks, in the prison community, consist of punishment and confiscation, and in the past, when discipline was rigorous, such risks were considerable. The research period at Pentonville, however, was one in which discipline was becoming progressively relaxed without any significant increase in the official supply of those goods and services which would improve the prisoners' material well-being.

In Pentonville there is no argot role corresponding to that of the *merchant* reported by Sykes in his Trenton study.[13] In the New Jersey State Prison it appears that the inmate code places considerable stress on the desirability of *giving* and at the same time deprecates the activities of the *merchant* or *pedlar* who sells when he should give. Balanced reciprocity in which the principle of equivalence is uppermost is apparently not classed as merchant activity. It seems necessary here to distinguish between reciprocal giving, or

[13] Sykes, *op. cit.*, p. 93 *et seq.*

barter, and selling for profit. In the maximum security prison, where the medium of exchange is tobacco rather than the currency of the realm, exchanges which are mutually agreeable to both sides may look like the exchange of gifts, but are, unless the transaction takes place between 'mates', of a fundamentally economic character. Neither in Maidstone nor Pentonville was there much evidence of barter, and the majority of transactions were conducted in tobacco. Nevertheless, prisoners can and do distinguish between what is a 'fair price' and what is 'ruthless exploitation'. At the economic level exploitation in contractual relationships is difficult if only because of the existence of competition. When exploitation does occur it is either because the exploited prisoner is a weak, inadequate personality or of feeble intellect, or more commonly, because economic power is overshadowed by coercion or the threat of it. The only argot role which comes near to corresponding with the New Jersey *merchant* is the *baron*, indeed the baron is the only role specifically recognized in the language of the prison. Both staff and inmates identify the baron who sells tobacco (or rather lends it at interest) as an undesirable; the staff because his activities are a threat to good order and discipline, and the inmates because of the extortionate overtones of his role.[14]

Because of the character of the rules, illicit activities are recognized as such by both staff and prisoners, but the term *'fiddling'* conveys accurately the lack of moral obloquy in the inmate attitude towards it. It is the term *baroning* which is the focus of concern, particularly on the part of the staff whose dogmatic belief is that tobacco baroning is the prime cause of violence and disorder among their captives. Seen from the custodial viewpoint, all fiddling and baroning is illicit, so that in one sense the structure of illicit economic institutions has very much the character of bootlegging during the Prohibition era—bootlegging rather than the traffic in narcotics, because whereas narcotics are physiologically destructive and socially

[14] Even when the baron does not 'extort' he is the object of the same diffuse feelings of disapproval which attach very closely to money-lenders and pawn-brokers in the community outside.

disapproved, the demand for alcohol was regarded as legitimate by the majority of normal citizens. For the prisoner, participation in this economic system serves not only to lessen his material deprivations but to modify the effects of his loss of autonomy. Because it is a system of behaviour with recognized means and ends he is able to exercise a limited but significant degree of choice; he is able to make decisions, and he is provided with an outlet for both intellectual skill and manual dexterity by the challenge to ingenuity which production and exchange presents.

The interdependence of individuals which this comparatively complex economic system creates is sufficient to transcend the difficulties of entering into face-to-face relationships and thereby communication with men in other parts of the prison becomes possible. Groups which might otherwise remain *incomunicado* are linked by runners, and routinized techniques of communication serve to buttress the structure of inmate society still further.

In contrast to baroning which is concerned solely with tobacco dealings and will be discussed under leadership, *fiddling* is regarded by prisoners as a wholly legitimate activity, the Prison Rules notwithstanding. Nevertheless, although transactions which occur in relation to 'fiddles' may be wholly concordant, the authorities view certain "fiddles" as serious, particularly those which involve the theft of food. In Trenton it appears that inmates state that 'the man stealing stuff from the institution is stealing from me.'. Even in Pentonville this is true, but not recognized. Food is issued and stored in measured quantities and when, for example, sugar is stolen, all that happens is that the tea and the rice pudding are less sweet—which in turn stimulates a greater demand for stolen sugar.

Strictly speaking, a distinction needs to be drawn between the tobacco baron and the man who provides other goods and services at an economic cost. The distinction is not always easy to draw because the dividing line between business enterprise which is successfully competitive and sheer economic exploitation or racketeering is narrow. Where the transaction involves simple exchange, e.g., payment for getting an extra shirt—no difficulties normally arise.

It is only when the transaction is protracted as in the case of gambling or tobacco debts that some additional device of enforcement becomes necessary.

Tobacco is at the centre of illicit enterprise in Pentonville, Maidstone and, indeed, almost every maximum security prison because the whole structure of the illicit economy depends upon it. Not only is it a consumption good in short supply (because it is sold at the normal market price in the canteen) but a currency as well. In this respect it has the character of a currency based upon a gold or silver standard, where currency is worth what the metal is worth. Prison earnings, being paid in credit form, must be converted into a medium of exchange if payments are to be made which cannot be effected by crude barter. Tobacco, like money, is portable, uniformly acceptable, of uniform quality, readily divisible and comes in convenient denominations. In this way the man who buys tobacco in the canteen which he does not intend to smoke is performing the same economic act as the man who cashes a cheque on his bank account.

There is little doubt that a certain amount of cash in currency notes of the realm circulates in Pentonville, too. Because a ten-shilling note is the smallest denomination, it has limited value for settling economic transactions, and is almost certainly limited to payment of bribes to 'bent screws'.

'Baroning', the loan of tobacco at interest, has been generally viewed by prison officials and prisoners alike as a consequence of low earnings and the prisoner's need for a smoke. Certainly the scarcity of tobacco as a consumption good—or rather, the difficulty of being able to afford it in reasonable quantity—is an important factor. But the payment of earnings in credit makes it equally important as a medium of exchange, and although increases in the basic wage together with the system of advance payment on reception may well lessen the new prisoner's chances of falling into the hands of a baron, the overall effect is slight. This is because of the demand for tobacco as a currency for use in a whole range of economic transactions, including gambling, which could not otherwise flourish.[15]

The precise structure of baroning is said to vary in detail from one prison to another, dependent upon the ease or otherwise of communication. Thus in Maidstone the barons operated on a cell house basis because the evenings were periods of association in which business could be easily transacted. In Pentonville where, with the exception of H Wing, association is severely limited, the barons are workshop based, for it is there that the best market opportunities occur.

In both Pentonville and Maidstone it was clear that not everyone associated with this particular form of illicit enterprise played an identical economic role. At the apex of the system are a few major barons—in Pentonville about ten—with access to primary sources of supply. It is to the major baron that the parcels of tobacco that are thrown over the wall, sometimes of as much as 25 oz. at a time, are consigned. He also has his contacts with prisoners on outside parties who can bring tobacco in, but among his most important sources is the so-called 'bent screw'. If, as is often the case, he has considerable financial resources outside, he is able to enjoy a relatively stable supply. To some extent he is in competition with the bent screw who also supplies individual prisoners, but under normal conditions the market is sufficiently large to allow both to operate without impinging upon the other. Not all the major barons have large resources of cash outside. By manipulation of their wives and relatives, those who are less well off may manage to raise sufficient to obtain a capital stock via a 'bent screw'. A pen-picture of such a baron comes from the following essay by a man with long years of prison experience:

He is mercenary minded, generally tough and has an energetic mind and a hard heart. Being thus, and being in possession of a great deal of tobacco this man indeed becomes a highly dangerous body. He has no money outside and intends to make it while he is in. His first joey (par-

[15] Increases in credit earnings, when the supply of illicit goods and services remains relatively constant, is likely to operate as an inflationary influence.

cel of tobacco) will in all probability be his only one . . . but sufficient to start him off. Having received the first consignment he proceeds to baron. This may take various forms.

He may lay out the tobacco at (as much as) 100% interest. An eighth will bring a quarter, a quarter a half and so on. On the other hand, he may re-sell the tobacco for cash. This kind of credit sale is frequently made and his profit on the whole joey may amount to a fiver or so. He is approached by another prisoner and the sale price is £1 per ounce the money to be sent to the holder (or his agent outside) *before* any tobacco is passed. The remaining (tobacco) will then be laid out at 100% and in time he will again be able to sell another load at £1 per ounce.

He may use the tobacco for other purposes. It may well be that he is a big eater, or has a sweet tooth. In this case part of the interest rate will pass on to someone in the kitchen. If he is that way inclined that he likes to look smart, then he will devote some interest to the stores where clothing is kept. The tobacco will allow him to have his cell cleaned by someone, have the first choice of library books; give him an 'in' to almost any sphere of the prison world where the majority only get by industry and good conduct.

Because their access to primary sources of supply is comparatively well organized, the major barons are able to supply a somewhat larger number of minor barons. These men tend to operate intermittently, again on a shop basis. Their motivations vary, and they are also frequently involved in bookmaking which is made possible by the existence of the major barons who, at a price, are prepared to underwrite their losses. In the words of one such minor baron:

The barons are quite active in the workshops. As there are many shades of feeling with regard to these I can only give my own opinion on the matter. In the first place, I must admit that I could be called a baron myself from time to time. I, like most inmates of my age (29), accept bets and lend tobacco. My surplus in the first place came from betting— football, boxing and horses. Over a period of a year I can show a profit of say 20 ounces.

Major barons tend to deal in tobacco in packet form which is readily divisible and easily portable, though minor barons from time to time convert it into 'roll ups', of which about forty can be made from an ounce. Minor barons normally have a clientele of about ten to fifteen men.

Another factor which varies is the actual 'retail price' of tobacco. Such variations depend on the extent to which communication problems result in each workshop constituting a separate market. Even in a given shop prices may vary. When one or two major barons begin an attempt to raise prices (either to increase their profits or to cover losses resulting from confiscation, bookmaking losses and so on) the number of minor barons tends to increase. The presence of these 'marginal' barons is sufficient to bring down the price to a new equilibrium level.

Not all, however, is pure profit, for apart from the barons themselves there are the *runners*. Because of the prison rule which lays down that no inmate may have more then 2 oz. at a time, it is necessary for the capital and the 'takings' to be carried by a number of other men. The runner in addition is the normal go-between for the barons and the bent screw, and is responsible for the transport of basic supplies from the point of entry to the baron. These latter tasks are particularly important in order that official suspicion should fall neither on the baron, nor, if he is dealing with one, on the bent screw.

Although it would be true to say that a majority of prisoners detest baroning, almost without exception they see it as inevitable, as an evil only capable of solution by an unlimited issue of free tobacco or a major increase in earnings. The often slender resources of wives are taxed by payments to barons' agents and some prisoners expressed disgust that the National Assistance payments which should be feeding and clothing families were going into the barons' pockets. A baron, who in fact denied being one because he claimed that barons were only interested in deals over £5 whereas he dealt in lesser sums, showed one of the research workers a letter from his wife in which she referred to '£40 he had promised to send her'. This man sold tobacco at 1½ oz. to the £1 and had in two years made a profit of £30, being owed a lot more. He normally got men to send money to his wife, either via *their* wives or from their private cash. He sometimes got his wife to write in to a particular man demanding 'the money that he owed her', the man then arranging payment via a special letter or via his wife.

When a baron leaves the prison, either on discharge or transfer, if he has any stock of tobacco he will endeavour to transform it into cash. Although this is seldom difficult, problems can arise when individuals defraud each other. Thus, just before he was due for discharge, Jackson,[16] a former hostel red-band—who had been turned off the job as a result of his tobacco dealings there—told another prisoner, Cartwright, that he had some tobacco to dispose of. Cartwright did not want it himself, but eventually found someone who did and instructed him to 'send it (payment money) to a man in the hostel'. The money was sent, but no tobacco materialized. Cartwright queried this with Jackson, who first denied that the hostel man had received the money, but then said that the tobacco belonged not to him after all, but to the hostel man, who was not prepared to produce it. Angry at being double-crossed, Cartwright started a fight, but as Jackson was a man of muscular physique he got the best of the day. Cartwright informed the staff of the fight but as he had been acting as a middleman he eventually left the prison under something of a cloud with the staff.

. . . . .

## Leadership, Stability and Conflict

Pentonville, like most large city prisons, is a place where beneath a surface calm runs a constant and dangerous undertow of inmate conflict. The surface, moreover, is marked frequently by the tell-tale ripples of physical violence in the obscurity below. For every fight between prisoners which is witnessed or comes to the notice of the staff [17] there are three or four others which are 'not witnessed by any-

[16] All names used throughout this book are fictitious.
[17] In 1959 there were thirty-six cases of assault on prisoners in which disciplinary action was taken.

one'. Conflict between prisoners represents one of the most serious threats to the inmate social system, not merely because it imperils the whole structure of co-operative illicit enterprise, but because when it rises above the level which the staff can tolerate, it produces greater problems for the individual prisoner. The staff must maintain 'good order and discipline', and although they may feel little sympathy for the weak prisoner who has fallen prey to the barons and still less for the bully who has at last met his match, disorder is an unfavourable reflection upon custodial competence. The solution is invariably to 'tighten up' by rigorous searching, workshop reallocation and cell transfers from one wing to another. Such measures normally include 'too many' rather than 'too few' individuals, and can wreck havoc with systematized arrangements within the inmate economy.

Conflict takes a variety of forms, of which the ostracism of inmates with pariah status is the least disturbing in that it takes the shape of non-cooperation rather than tangibly expressed hostility. Next in order of seriousness comes the individual 'punch-up'. The 'punch-up' is normally a spontaneous occurrence: a word or gesture acts as a spark in a potentially volatile situation in the workshop, a recess, or on the exercise yard. Most serious of all are the premeditated 'goings over' of individuals by small groups of men who are the bodyguard of a gang leader, and the semi-ritualized gang fights which occur between rival groups contending for power in inmate society.

. . . . .

In Pentonville the threshold of violence is comparatively low, for not only does the population contain a significant minority of aggressive psychopaths but most prisoners are familiar with the cult of violence which is currently in vogue among young professional criminals outside and well represented in the prison. Tensions build up easily in the prison, particularly after days of rain and inside exercise. But while the incidence of individual 'punch-ups' tends to fluctuate, systematic 'goings over' of debtors or others who have failed to keep bargains and gang fights occur with some regularity.

Gang fights occur not only in relation to power struggles in the prison, but are frequently an extension of group conflicts *outside*. The bone of contention outside may be rivalry in some criminal activity. It may, however, be a long-standing feud arising out of grassing or informing to the police, or the seduction of a wife or girl friend. As in most human communities, the ultimate equilibrium of the system will depend upon a balance of the forces contending for power; and power, in inmate society, is based sometimes upon consensus, sometimes upon external constraint, and frequently upon a combination of the two. The physical, social and psychological deprivations of imprisonment undoubtedly stimulate among most prisoners behaviour which is designed to minimize them; at the same time the prison contains men with strong drives towards controlling other men and in so doing satisfying many of their inner psychological needs.

Because the inmate community is more than an inchoate mass, but contains a range of contending elements, this process may be best understood by a consideration of the phenomenon of leadership which the conditions of maximum security inevitably precipitate.

. . . . .

The *form* that leadership takes varies considerably. A leader may be the acknowledged head of a group of men (often known as a gang) who makes autocratic decisions about attitudes and behaviour to be adopted towards the staff or other prisoners. Alternatively a leader may be merely *primus inter pares* among three or four other prisoners all of whom enjoy the respect of a wider circle of acquaintances.

The *function* of leadership also varies. It may be directed towards long-term ends such as the provision of an emotional bulwark against the pressures of the prison authority by the maintenance of emotional solidarity—the 'we' continually opposed to 'they'. In so doing, inmate leadership helps to lessen the pains of imprisonment by constantly reasserting the arbitrary injustices of the prison régime and the immutable values of inmate culture which, come what may, cannot, it is believed, be eradicated by the staff. Alternatively, the function of leadership may be to enable individual inmates to combine in the effective exploitation of their fellows whom the prison authorities are normally unable (and sometimes unwilling) to protect. The effects of this type of leadership are broadly dysfunctional for inmate solidarity as a whole, for they give rise to the development of other 'protective' associations who frequently exploit in their turn. To the extent to which such leaders exist and generate internecine feuds, inmate solidarity as a whole in the face of custodial authority is appreciably diminished.

Sykes, in his analysis of Trenton, distinguishes between 'cohesive' and 'alienative' responses in the face of imprisonment. The cohesive response is an action or series of actions which is collectivist in character in that it is directed towards the interests of prisoners *as a whole*. The alienative response, on the other hand, is highly individualistic in character and directed towards the satisfactions of one individual or small group exploiting both staff and other prisoners as the need arises. Given this, two ideal types of leader can be distinguished: the *'Robin Hood'* and the *'Robber Baron'*.[18] Both types are 'troublemakers' as far as the prison authorities are concerned; nevertheless, the 'trouble' they create varies appreciably.

The *Robin Hood* is considered by the mass of the prisoner population to be a major asset in the task of minimizing the pains of imprisonment. The leader is a strong-willed man, wise in prison ways, committed to the inmate code of minimal co-operation with the staff but careful never to provoke or bring down trouble upon himself or his associates. He is benevolent, sympathetic, and has many of the marks of a genuine altruist. Such a man was Smith, a 40-year-old club owner with ten previous convictions and six previous sentences. He was well above average in intelligence, a resilient, well-integrated personality, not over-enthusiastic about work, but shrewd in pursuing his objectives. His flair for organization and

[18] The term 'baron' in this context, i.e., *Robber Baron,* should not be confused with the term *Tobacco* Baron. Although some tobacco barons are also robber barons, the terms are not synonymous.

control, manifested outside by his involvement with organized crime, was turned in prison to large-scale bookmaking. He dominated the prison by his intelligence and wealth, and although suspected of trafficking with an officer, almost certainly made his tobacco profits 'inside'. Though despising 'mugs' and 'tearways', it is likely that he used the latter as lieutenants in his complex system of controlling the operations of bookmaking, as many of those closely associated with him were aggressive psychopathic individuals. His main claim to popular status was in helping unfortunate prisoners—by arranging for presents to be sent to wives to assist in matrimonial reconciliations, or to children on their birthdays. A wealthy man outside the prison, he would, if desired, make the services of his own solicitor available to other prisoners without one of their own. In all this, of course, he furthered his own self-interest—other prisoners would be glad to do his work in the workshops, to perform personal services for him. In his relations with the staff he was 'polite and inoffensive', keeping well out of trouble.

Smith's role in the prison community was essentially cohesive. For prisoners he represented a tower of strength—'cleverer than all these screws put together'. He advised and controlled, the extent of his power and influence being sufficient to minimize many of the disruptive forces operative in the inmate social system. His economic interests gave him a vested interest in the stability, not only of the inmate sub-system, but of the social system of the prison as a whole. Although the staff disliked him (jealous of his wealth and resentful of his intelligence in some cases) and regarded him as an undesirable exploiter of other prisoners, both he and they had a mutual interest in order and stability. . . . Superiority of brain, and the ability to call upon brawn when necessary, gave Smith an unusual amount of power. It was based, however, upon *loyalty* rather than fear, his good and generous deeds making many men his permanent moral debtors. The staff frequently alleged, "Smith is at the back of all the trouble on the wing at the moment', without any tangible evidence; the effect of their belief was to reinforce Smith's status in the eyes of his fellows as the 'master mind'.

The *Robber Baron* is a very different sort of man. He is recognized by prisoners as an exploiter, a man whom they would rather do without. In many cases he is actually a tobacco baron or a bookmaker but frequently he is no more than an extortionate bully who demands protection payments or feudal services from those inmates unfortunate enough to come under his influence. His role corresponds very closely to that of the *gorillas* and *merchants* of the New Jersey State Prison.[19] He tends to be younger than the Robin Hood, to resort to violence with some frequency and on account of this is to be feared by most other inmates. Furthermore, his activities tend to be less consistently organized and to be concentrated upon short-run rather than long-term objectives.

The Robber Baron, then, is not a leader who can make moral claims upon his followers, but relies upon coercion and fear. It is doubtful whether he is a 'gang' leader in that the term gang implies organization and permanence which is seldom characteristic of the group of men he attracts, the term 'near-group' being more appropriate in that it expresses the unstable and ephemeral nature of the bond between him and his immediate followers. Sykes writes of the disappearance of well-organized gangs in Trenton leaving:

. . . a few cliques . . . loosely held together and small in size consisting of a dominant figure and several sycophants—an association of coercive exploiters . . . (which) poses a fearful threat for the general inmate population: as one prisoner has said, 'If you decide to fight one of them you have to fight them all'.[20]

Compare this with the statement of a prisoner in Pentonville:

Today there are no really big barons, only about 12 of the lesser variety in the whole place. They can't do anything unless they go round in a gang—they are the really dangerous types in the prison. They come in with a reputation and others flock around them bathing in their reflected glory. The leaders are so-called villains, and like to think they're great shakes but in fact they can't do anything alone. They are really afraid of trouble. The danger of them is that *if you have a square fight with a*

[19] Sykes, *op. cit.*, pp. 90 *et seq.*
[20] *Op. cit.*, p. 92.

*gang member you have to go on and fight all the gang in turn if they feel like it.*

The correspondence of these two statements is remarkable: it is noteworthy that in both prisons there is a widespread belief that these men are cowards, and that they succeed either because other prisoners are even bigger cowards, or because they operate in groups.

The dichotomy between Robin Hoods and Robber Barons is to some extent a reflection of the maturing pattern of behaviour exhibited by men of violent proclivities as they get older. The older men exert their power and influence by more subtle means than the younger, and although they may be able to give a good account of themselves in a fight, violence is frequently delegated to their younger sycophants. Many older prisoners fear the younger elements simply on account of their superior physical strength; one prisoner (a confidence trickster in his 60s) commented: 'The prison is run by young thugs. The only way to adjust in here is to become a vegetable, otherwise you will be in trouble sooner or later.' Another, aged just over 70, said he loathed '. . . the young tearaways in here who rule the prison by force. Even the officers are reluctant to challenge them unless absolutely necessary.' By and large, these older men steer well clear of the toughs, and are experienced enough not to get into debt with tobacco barons and bookmakers, quite often because they have the kind of job in the prison which carries many 'perks' and allows them to perform services for other inmates for which they are paid in tobacco. For those men who do become indebted to the barons and bookmakers, the solution is more difficult.

Not all the Robber Barons are involved in economic enterprise, but operate in other areas. For example, in H Wing, Higgins assumed control soon after he had been transferred from the main prison. Higgins was 27 years old, serving three years for robbery, with sentences totalling four and a half years already behind him. Outside he was a lorry driver with many criminal associates. Lacking in academic education, he was shrewd and experienced rather than innately intelligent, a powerful bully who was not afraid to use force in the last extremity. He was well adjusted to his criminal life but tended to be suspicious and narcissistic. He sold tobacco but was not a tobacco baron in the strict sense. His concern was to make sure that other prisoners performed services for him. For example, he gave a man a contraband wireless for nothing on condition that he could borrow it back whenever he wanted it. Various prisoners were only too eager to clean his cell for him, and although the usual amount payable for such a service was ⅛ oz. tobacco, he paid a quarter.

In his activities on the wing, Higgins had the moral and tactical support of Jones, a 35-year-old aggressive psychopath serving an eight-year sentence for manslaughter. Large and physically powerful, Jones had a record of violence in and out of prison and was feared and 'respected' by staff and prisoners alike. His psychopathology was complex, and apart from sharing in the control of wing activities, e.g., of who should have access to games, which TV programmes should be chosen, etc., he would exert control over his sycophants by literally using them as furniture. Higgins had established his supremacy on the wing by a series of four big fights with the man who had previously held this position; nevertheless his rule did not preclude the existence of other strong men whose interests were more limited. Such a man was Charles, a 40-year-old scrap metal dealer serving four years for factory breaking and receiving, with nine prison sentences behind him. A violent, quick-tempered man with a taste for high living outside (mainly gambling), he had a reputation among the staff as a troublemaker. Other prisoners described him as a *stirrer* rather than a leader in that he got others to do the dirty work for him. The Chief Officer described him as 'a man who makes the bullets for other people to fire'. His group had no direct interest in racketeering, but merely wanted to dominate the wing; for example, if they wanted to play snooker other people had to give up the table; their food always had to be served first and they had to have the best seats for TV.

The motivations of men like Higgins, Jones and Charles are complex in that while they wish to lessen the pains of imprisonment by getting other prisoners to make their life easier, the desire to exert power for its own sake is an important component. Just as they build up a reputation for toughness outside, so too in the prison 'rep' (to use a convenient American hoodlum term) is important. Indeed, a man's reputation *outside* would diminish unless he continued to act in a dominant and aggressive manner *inside*.

In reality, the prisoner must steer a course between the Prison Rules and the Prisoners' Rules, and the task is frequently difficult. The prison as a whole is territorially divided between wings, workshops and exercise yards, and in each of these areas inmate leadership will be exercised.

The 'fiddler' or business man in the prison who supplies some illicit good or service is *not necessarily* a Robber Baron; indeed, many of the economic transactions of the prison are conducted without discord or acrimony. When the Robber Baron involves himself in economic activities it is invariably those of a speculative, risk-taking nature, in which the stakes are high and the element of genuine reciprocity minimal—such as tobacco baroning and bookmaking. His activities tend to be diffuse, relatively localized—in the shop or on the wing—and to be subject to the limitations imposed by the activities of others like him.

Many of the men in this category are not leaders in the sense that they exert power and influence in a consistent way; they have little popular support based upon consensus and the constraints which they attempt to impose on others are frequently challenged. More properly they can be classified as *toughs*. Such a man was Nelson, a 28-year-old man serving three years and with a long history of approved school, Borstal and prison behind him. He described himself as a professional criminal, saying, 'Work makes you ill, laying about don't'. Outside prison his criminal contacts were extensive. His personality approximated towards that of the aggressive psychopath; he was invariably hostile to authority, suspicious and greedy, but in many ways insecure. Both staff and prisoners considered him to be one of the most dangerous men in the prison. (He had attacked a prison officer on a previous sentence and believed that he was victimized for ever after.)

All prisoners are officially warned on their cell information cards not to become involved in tobacco or similar transactions; but for many this is a pious hope. Once involved, and unable to pay, the debtor is in a serious position. Not all tobacco barons immediately order their henchmen to administer a 'going over'; after all, what they want primarily is the tobacco. The threat of violence is often sufficient to get a debtor to pay off some of his debt, but if it is a large one—of more than 3 or 4 oz.—he will never pay it off entirely. One resort is to apply for protection under Rule 36 of the Prison Rules, whereby the Governor may authorize arrangements for the prisoner to have non-associated labour in his cell. At the end of one month, this arrangement must be approved by the Visiting Justices. Rule 36, however, is seldom an adequate solution, for neither the Governer— nor for that matter the Visiting Justices—are disposed to protect a man under the rule if he will not disclose the identity of his suspected assailants. Few prisoners can afford to flout the Prisoners' Code and 'grass' in this way; for one thing, this would almost certainly invite vengeance and, for another, the prisoner may be genuinely ignorant of the precise identity of his assailants. His creditor will, as part of the psychological terror, deliberately keep him in ignorance of who has been delegated to carry out the attack.

The remaining solutions must be sought by the prisoner himself. He may, in extremity, injure himself or swallow some object in order to be hospitalized, and although instances of this do occur, they tend to be solutions of men of unstable personality. More reasonable, and in the long run more effective, is the solution of self-help. As Sykes cogently observes, the presence of home-made weapons discovered by the staff in the process of searching is partially accounted for by the prevalence of 'gorillas'; they are weapons of self-defence in the inmate community rather than offensive weapons to be used against the staff.[21] To some extent self-help is most effective when collectively organized, but it would seem that defensive activity presents more problems than the reverse.

Because many of the social controls in the inmate social system tend to be based upon external constraint rather than internal con-

[21] Sykes, *op. cit.*, p. 92.

sensus, the equilibrium of the system tends to be symbiotic, resembling the primitive world of nature. Just as in an aquarium, where one species tends to prey upon another while other species are allowed to live in peace, a balance is achieved when the predatory species prey equally upon one another. So, too, in the prison, violence and exploitation are kept within limits by the presence of rival groups who co-exist for the most part below rather than above the threshold of violence and overt conflict. When violetnce begins to assert itself it may be checked by violence, and in such situations can be perceived the beginnings of the metamorphosis of the *tough* into the *Robin Hood*.

Such a man was Brown, a 27-year-old unskilled labourer who had achieved some distinction as an amateur boxer, then serving a five-year sentence for defrauding the G.P.O. Although his outside criminal contacts were extensive he differed from the normal *tough* pattern in that he was a hard worker. An illiterate man of primitive and aggressive feelings, he had little control over them, and he admitted to the research worker that he was frightened by his own increasing violence.

In the prison he attempted to limit the powers of the robber barons by what were (for the prison authorities) unorthodox means, i.e., by the use of force. Even the Governor had to admit that Brown kept order among prisoners, but became ambivalent as the number of his assaults on other prisoners increased. When, in an uncontrolled moment, he let fly at a prison officer and was taken before the Visiting Justices, another prison officer commented that he 'hoped the V.C. wouldn't be too tough and turn him against authority. *He is a good man at keeping order in the prison.*' It so happened that he was not harshly dealt with, but unfortunately continued to be violent towards other prisoners. Nevertheless, his coercive activities were *positively* oriented; for example, when a fight broke out, a (weak-willed) prisoner was told by an officer to ring the alarm bell, which he did. Brown 'gave him a belting' for this quite flagrant violation of the inmate code. While the staff tended to perceive Brown as a nuisance when he got out of hand, prisoners regarded him as a man who, though wise to avoid, nevertheless maintained justice in inmate society.

## Suggestions for Further Reading

R. G. ANDRY, *The Short-Term Prisoner* (London: Stevens, 1963). Although mainly a psychological study, this has some valuable background information on the social characteristics of prisoners which is directly comparable with the data for long-term prisoners in Pentonville.

D. M. DOWNES, *The Delinquent Solution* (London: Routledge and Kegan Paul, 1966). Subtitled "A Study in Subcultural Theory," this book sets English experience with criminal behavior against the context of American theorizing about delinquent and, in particular, working-class "subcultures."

A. B. DUNLOP and S. MC CABE, *Young Men in Detention Centres* (London: Routledge and Kegan Paul, 1965). The majority of Pentonville prisoners were over 30 at the time of the Morris study, although the modal age was 25, and most of the men were "old" offenders. A comparison with younger prisoners is therefore of considerable value, and this study provides interesting details.

BARBARA WOOTTON, *Social Science and Social Pathology* (London: Allen and Unwin, 1959). An excellent general survey of all aspects of criminological research findings in England up to 1958. The emphasis is on the methodological strengths and weaknesses of this work, and on the logic of the practical conclusions thought to follow from it.

# ❧The Home and the School

J. W. B. DOUGLAS

*In 1946 the mothers of all babies born during the first week of March were contacted eight weeks after delivery by Dr. Douglas and his colleagues in England, Wales, and Scotland. Interviews were successfully completed with 90 percent of them. Of these 13,687 mothers, 7,287 completed a questionnaire dealing mainly with the availability of maternity services and the use they had made of them, and 6,400 replied to questions on medical expenditures and other costs associated with the birth of their babies. A report on these findings was published in 1948.[1]*

*Originally, it was not intended that this should be the first stage of a long-term follow-up series of inquiries, but since the investigators found that they were in possession of a fully representative sample of children from all types of homes and all parts of Britain it was decided to follow them through for at least part of their future. A sample of 5,362 children was selected from the original sample for further research, and by 1948 the sample had dwindled to 5,005 and by 1950 to 4,921. But there was valuable information on what had by now happened to them during the first few years of life, and in 1958 a further*

[1] J. W. B. Douglas and G. Rowntree, *Maternity in Great Britain* (London: Oxford University Press, 1948).

SOURCE: J. W. B. Douglas, *The Home and the School: A Study of Ability and Attainment in the Primary School,* Chapters 6 and 7 (pp. 39–59). Copyright © 1964 by J. W. B. Douglas. Reprinted by permission of MacGibbon and Kee.

*report was published giving details of their experiences—accidents, illness, toilet training, parental care, etc.—as seen against the background of stable or broken homelife in the different social classes.*[2]

*By the summer of 1957, 623 of the original 5,362 children had died or moved abroad. There were left in England and Wales 4,195 children and 544 in Scotland. It was decided to study the educational experiences of only the English and Welsh children. Full information was available for 3,418 of these and partial information for 657, leaving 120 for whom there was no information. In spite of these losses the evidence showed that for most inquiry purposes the sample was still reasonably representative of the general population. Special school records had been kept of them and medical reports were available. At eight years and three months they were given a picture intelligence test and sentence completion, reading, and vocabulary tests. In England, primary education is completed at the end of the academic year in which a child reaches his eleventh birthday. All children sit the so-called 11+ examinations for entrance to secondary school during the year, and on the basis of the standard attained are awarded places in the secondary grammar, the secondary technical, and the secondary modern schools. The children included in Dr. Douglas's survey were also tested immediately before they sat their 11+ examinations. The reading and vocabulary tests were repeated, and they completed a mixed verbal and nonverbal intelligence test and an arithmetic test.*

*Throughout the period from 1946, health visitors and school nurses had visited the homes of the children on an average of once a year. In addition to recording accidents, hospital admissions, and absences from school of more than a week's duration, these visits provided information about the educational aspirations which parents had for their children and about the careers they had in mind for them. This information provided the background to the analysis made in the selection from the report published here. Thus although the emphasis is on the child at 11+, the classification of parents in*

[2] J. W. B. Douglas and J. M. Blomfield, *Children under Five* (London: Allen and Unwin, 1958).

*terms of the standards of care which they provided and the kind of encouragement which they gave their children, was made by reference to data collected over a period of eleven years; and in this sense it may be said to represent long-standing differences.*

*It should be understood that attitude surveys as normally understood were not employed in the three longitudinal studies by Douglas. As far as possible, the researchers relied upon objective measures, tests of the children, and easily recorded data on their circumstances, accidents, illness, size of the family, father's occupation, and so on. Subjective information was obtained, of course, but from the health visitors and the teachers rather than directly from the parents. This reduces the comparability which the work might otherwise have had with other surveys of the effect of parental encouragement in children's educational performance in, say, America. But because of its continuity through eleven years of the children's lives, J. W. B. Douglas's work on behalf of the Population Investigation Committee of the London School of Economics, the Society of Medical Officers of Health, and the Institute of Child Health, University of London will remain a most valuable contribution to the sociology of education for a long time to come.*

In this study we have no direct knowledge of the early influence of parents on their children's attitudes to learning, and can infer this only from what is known of their social origins and education, and of the level of skill they attain in their jobs. When, in an earlier book, the growth and health of these children was described, a social classification was used that was based on their fathers' jobs alone. They were divided into nine 'occupational groups', ranging from the children of professional workers to the children of unskilled labourers. There were wide differences in the amount of illness, and the rate of growth, among these nine groups of children, also in the use that their parents made of the medical services. The main distinction lies between the children of the non-manual workers and those of the manual workers. The former have, on the average, relatively little infectious illness in early childhood, they enjoy excellent standards of care at home and their mothers take them regularly to the child welfare centres and in general make good use of the available medical services. They have in other words what may be regarded as a middle class pattern of upbringing. In contrast, the manual working class children are more often ill, particularly with respiratory tract infections, and their mothers are seen by the health visitors as giving low standards of care to their children and homes, as making relatively little use of the child welfare centres and as often failing to have their children immunised against diphtheria.

It was originally intended to use the same nine occupational groups in this educational study. It soon became clear, however, that these groups were fluctuating and ill-defined. Some of this instability arose from the difficulty of establishing with accuracy the degree of skill used in particular jobs; job descriptions were often imprecise in spite of checking, and sometimes grossly misleading, so that in the light of further information 12 per cent of the original job codings had to be altered. But apart from this, job changes were frequent, and over the eleven years of this survey 43 per cent of families moved out of their original occupational groups, and some passed through several different groups.

This large volume of occupational movement stems in part from the relatively large number of groups into which the families were divided; there were nine groups instead of the five which the Registrar General uses routinely in his analyses of mortality. The greatest amount of change, however, is among the manual workers, who frequently move from semi-skilled to skilled occupations or vice versa; and so even the Registrar General's classification, which is largely based on the criterion of skill, would turn out to be fluctuating and impermanent when applied to a logitudinal study of this kind.

The survey started soon after the war and it might be thought that the greater part of the changes in employment that were recorded would be in the immediately succeeding years and represent an adjustment to peace-time conditions, but this was not so. The amount of change between the nine groups used at the beginning of this study was relatively steady from year to year, at a level of approximately 6 per cent. Some groups, for example professional or salaried workers, become more stable as time passes, recruiting from the younger men and losing mainly through retirement. Others, for example the black-coated wage earners or agricultural workers, show an even greater rate of change at the end of the survey than at the beginning. The main direction of change is upward, but there is a semi-permeable barrier between the non-manual and the manual groups across which, during the whole eleven years, only 5 per cent moved up and 3 per cent down.

Before going further with this discussion of how to classify these families we shall look at the unemployed; these are few in number but important because of the state of poverty in which they live and the signs of deprivation in their children. Unemployment among the fathers was 0.9 per cent in 1950, increasing to 2.9 per cent in 1957. Virtually all prolonged unemployment was a result of mental or physical illness or handicap, and the families were often profoundly affected. They lived in the most unsuitable and overcrowded homes, showed many other signs of poverty and were usually supported by the wages earned by the wives, who worked for long hours away from their homes and children.

Since these fathers were unemployed because they were ill rather than because they were mentally dull there is no reason why their children should do worse in the tests and in the secondary selection examinations than other children coming from similarly deprived homes. There is here no special element of inherited subnormality to take into account. But in fact they do considerably worse; they make an average score at eight years of 44.38 and, at eleven, of 44.47. These compare with average scores of 46.88 and 46.00 for the children of unskilled labourers at these ages. Seven per cent of the unskilled labourers' children go to grammar schools as compared with only 3 per cent of the children of the unemployed, and the teachers report that the latter are lazy and inattentive in school and that their parents take little interest in their progress. It may be that the key to their backwardness lies in worries and anxieties at home.

Families that move up or down the social scale have the characteristics and aspirations of the group they are joining rather than of the one they have left; this holds also for the ability of their children as measured by our tests and the results of the 11+ examinations. Children in families that are moving up have higher measured ability than those they leave behind though rather less than those they join. They also improve their test scores between the ages of eight and eleven years and if this improvement is maintained will soon eliminate their present slight handicap in the group they have joined. The reverse is true for the children in families that have moved down.

It seems, then, that the occupational changes of the eleven years of this survey have reshuffled the families by the social origins and education of the parents and, at second remove, by the intelligence of their children. It is likely that this process will continue in future years, and for this reason alone the father's occupation is an unsatisfactory criterion of social status for our present purpose. There is considerable sociological interest in observing the extent of movement between occupations, but this is not the main aim of this study —we wish to have a more stable means of summarising the social status of the families, which will also enable us to group together families of similar aspirations and standards.

The instability of occupations is not the only reason for abandoning them as a criterion of social status. It is, of course, inconvenient to have social categories that fluctuate and contain, at any chosen time, many families destined to move up or down and already showing some of the characteristics of the social group they will eventually join. This can only blur social differences. In addition, however, the boundaries of the categories are ill-defined and become more so as methods of payment—which allow salaried workers to be distinguished from clerical wage earners—change. An occupational classification can also be misleading in other ways; for example, there are in this survey several manual workers whose occupations give an entirely false impression of the opportunities of their children who are maintained at boarding schools by grandparents or godfathers.

A further serious criticism of a purely occupational classification is that it applies only to the fathers. We cannot afford to ignore the background of the mothers when looking at the educational progress of their children; they make an equal contribution with the fathers to inherited ability and possibly a greater one to attitudes to learning. In ambitious working class households it is not unusual to find that the mother comes from a middle class family and supplies the drive and incentive for her children to do well at school.

The education of both the parents is known and also the types of family in which they were each brought up. We will now see how far the social background and education of each parent relates to the views expressed by the mothers on their children's education. As our contacts were solely with the mothers it might be expected that the views they expressed would be more closely associated with their own education and origins than with their husbands'. This, however, was not so; the views expressed, for example, by mothers brought up in working-class families and educated at elementary schools, who were married to men with middle-class origins and secondary education, were exactly the same as those expressed by mothers with middle class origins and secondary education who were married to men brought up in working-class families and educated at elementary schools. Each group wanted their children on the average to leave school at sixteen years and eight months and each showed the same level of interest in their children's school progress. Moreover the level of their aspirations fell exactly between those of the two most contrasting groups; namely parents with entirely middle-class origins and secondary education on the one hand and those with entirely working-class origins and elementary education on the other.

The influence of the mothers' education and social backgrounds is also evident when we look at the average test scores of their children and performance in the secondary selection examinations; this influence is as strong as that of the fathers' education and social backgrounds, but no stronger. We know that for many young children it is the early contacts with their mothers that are likely to have the greatest influence on learning, and at later ages, too, it is often the mother who is more concerned than the father with school problems, and has the closest contact with the teachers. Because of this it seemed that among the survey children the mothers' influence on performance in school and in the tests might transcend the fathers'. That it exerts no more than an equal influence may perhaps be explained by the tendency for people to marry those with similar standards and ambitions. At any rate these observations show that it would be unwise to ignore the social origins and standard of education of the mothers when devising a new social classification.

The families were then grouped in the following way. First, those with a predominantly 'middle class' background, that is to say one of the parents was brought up in a non-manual worker's family *and* went to a secondary school, and the other had at least one of these characteristics; second, those with a purely working-class background, where both parents came from manual workers' families and received only an elementary school education; third, those who showed some middle class characteristics but did not fit into the first group.

When these three classes of families are further divided by the nature of the husband's present occupation a clear picture emerges. The children of non-manual workers fall into two main groups which have considerably different average scores in the eight- and eleven-year tests: those whose parents have middle class origins and secondary school education form a group which, on the average, make high scores whether their fathers are in the professions, in salaried employment, in blackcoated work or are self-employed; the remainder, whose parents may be said to deviate in their upbringing and education from the middle class pattern, make considerably lower average scores. The children from the first group not only make relatively high scores in the eight- and eleven-year tests, but also work hard in class and do conspicuously well in the 11+ examinations, getting more grammar school places than would be expected from their measured ability. In contrast, those from the second group, whose parents deviate from the middle class pattern, are less interested in their work and do relatively less well in the 11+ examinations. These differences in the performance of the children are reflected in the interests and aspirations of their parents. For these reasons the non-manual workers are grouped into two classes, the 'upper middle class' and the 'lower middle class'. Upper class and lower class are phrases we dislike, but in practice they give a convenient short description of these two groups. In making this division the employers and the self-employed are treated in the same way as the rest of the non-manual workers.

The manual working class families also split naturally into two groups. First, those in which one or both parents come from a middle class family, or have been to secondary schools. The great majority of these are skilled workers and we call them the 'upper manual working class'. Second, those in which both parents were brought up in working class families and had only an elementary school education; these we call the 'lower manual working class'. The latter may be regarded as wholly manual working class in origin, whereas the upper manual working class families deviate from this pattern. The lower manual working class children consistently show a substantial decline in test scores between eight and eleven years, and this is so whether the father is in skilled, semi-skilled or unskilled employment.

This division into four social classes (the upper and lower middle classes and the upper and lower manual working classes) has the great virtue for this study that it provides relatively stable groups that include essentially the same families whether the classification is made on the information available at the beginning of the survey or the end of it. Some assessments of these families are given in Table 1. . . .

There are considerable differences, as mentioned already, in the average test scores made by children in these four social classes. The upper middle class children, at eleven years, make an average score of 56.99; the lower middle class 53.88; the upper manual working class 50.05; the lower manual working class 47.55. It might be thought that the social class differences in test performance would be greatest in the tests which measured the level of achievement in

*Table 1.*

|  | MIDDLE CLASS MOTHERS | | MANUAL WORKING CLASS MOTHERS | |
|  | UPPER % | LOWER % | UPPER % | LOWER % |
|---|---|---|---|---|
| Highest standards of infant care | 53.1 | 37.0 | 22.1 | 15.1 |
| Highest standards of infant management | 66.2 | 49.4 | 34.5 | 28.1 |
| Good use of medical services | 78.9 | 67.4 | 54.2 | 42.4 |
| High interest in school progress | 41.7 | 21.7 | 11.4 | 5.0 |
| Desires grammar school place | 73.3 | 73.3 | 57.7 | 48.8 |
| Late school leaving wished | 77.6 | 40.7 | 21.7 | 12.9 |
| At least four of the above | 81.0 | 58.0 | 34.6 | 19.6 |

school subjects, but this is not so. These are similar differences between the social classes in each type of test that was used, and a slight suggestion that the lower manual working class children are underachievers and that the upper middle class children are over-achievers. The intelligence test used at eleven years was in two parts, one of which was given pictorially (and so did not involve the understanding of words), whereas the other involved seeing similarities between the meanings of words. There is a very slight tendency for the middle class children to do better in the 'verbal' than in the 'non-verbal' part of this intelligence test, whereas the manual working class children do worse in the 'verbal' part. This is mentioned because it confirms the findings of some other studies, but standing alone it might well be explained as a chance effect because the differences are so slight.

At eleven years the average test scores made by children in the four social classes differ more widely than they did at eight. The two middle class groups come closer together and move further away from the manual working classes; this shows itself in intelligence tests as well as in tests of school achievement.

It is well known that when tests are repeated after an interval, children who make low scores tend, on the average, to improve their position, whereas those who make high scores tend to deteriorate. It would therefore be expected that the middle class children who, on the average, score highly at eight would show a drop in score at eleven, and that the manual working class children who make low scores at eight would show an improvement; but, as has already been mentioned, the middle class children improve their scores and the working class children deteriorate—this holds at each level of ability. By the time he is eleven, the clever manual working class child has fallen behind the middle class child of similar ability at eight years, and equally the backward manual working class child shows less improvement between eight and eleven years than the backward middle class child. The consistency of these differences is shown in Table 2.

*Table 2.*

| | MIDDLE CLASS | | MANUAL WORKING CLASS | |
| | UPPER. | LOWER | UPPER | LOWER |
| SCORE AT EIGHT YEARS | CHANGE IN SCORE 8–11 YEARS | CHANGE IN SCORE 8–11 YEARS | CHANGE IN SCORE 8–11 YEARS | CHANGE IN SCORE |
|---|---|---|---|---|
| 40 or below | * | +2.52 | +0.50 | +0.68 |
| 41–45 | * | +1.84 | +0.90 | −0.23 |
| 46–50 | +3.44 | +2.38 | +0.59 | +0.02 |
| 51–55 | +1.81 | +1.71 | +0.19 | −0.78 |
| 56–60 | +1.52 | +0.62 | −0.81 | −2.27 |
| 60 and over | −2.32 | −1.94 | −3.17 | −4.60 |

* Fewer than 20 children in these groups.

+ = improvement      − = deterioration

Social class differences in secondary selection are marked. Fifty-four per cent of upper middle class children, but only 11 per cent of lower manual working class children, go to grammar schools; and not all of the poor achievement of the working class children is explained by their lower measured ability. If we compare secondary selection within groups of children whose eleven-year test scores are similar, the middle class children are consistently at an advantage until very high levels of performance are reached. With children in the top two per cent of ability, social background is unimportant, but below this it has a considerable influence on their chances of going to grammar schools. As an illustration consider children who score between 55 and 57 in the tests; among them grammar school places are awarded at the age of eleven to 51 per cent from the upper middle classes, 34 per cent from the lower middle, 21 per cent from the upper manual, and 22 per cent from the lower manual working classes.

The reason for these differences may lie in the personal qualities of the pupils (their industry and behaviour in class) or in the attitude of their parents, who may give them much or little encouragement in their work. At the present time these inequalities may be inevitable; but they still result in a considerable waste of ability which may be conserved in the future when attitudes to education have changed. It is not an idle exercise to work out how many grammar school places would be needed if the opportunities for selection which are enjoyed by upper middle class children applied to the population at large.

If at each level of measured ability at eleven all children, whatever their home background, had the same chance of getting to grammar school as the upper middle class children, places would be needed for 27 per cent of children rather than for 21 per cent.

In the regions where there is relatively good provision of grammar school places, the lower middle class children do just as well for each level of measured ability as the upper middle class in the selection examinations. In contrast the upper manual working class children get 15 per cent fewer places in grammar schools than would be got by a group of upper middle class children with a similar distribution of test scores, and the lower manual working class children get 28 per cent fewer. It is particularly the children of just above average ability who are at a disadvantage.

When grammar school places are in short supply the upper middle class children are as likely to get grammar school places as they would be if they lived in more favoured regions. The main effect of the shortage falls on the lower middle and the manual working class children. The lower middle class children living in these poorly favoured areas get 28 per cent fewer places than an equivalent group of upper middle class children, the upper manual working class children get 40 per cent fewer, and the lower manual working class children get 48 per cent fewer. Among the latter even the relatively clever children—with scores of 61 and over—get 15 per cent fewer places than an equivalent group of upper middle class children. It seems that when grammar school places are hard to come by, it is particularly the manual working class child who is affected.

Grammar school awards are of course seldom made on the results of intelligence tests and school achievement tests alone. A director of education might think it unjustifiable to send a relatively able child to a grammar school if his chances of success were small through lack of staying power and ambition. And this view is especially likely when the available number of grammar school places is strictly limited. Perhaps manual working class children fail to get the number of grammar school places that their measured ability would justify, because many of them lack these and other qualities needed for later academic success; qualities, moreover, which our relatively short and specialised tests do not measure. This explanation is untenable in face of the regional differences that have just been described, unless one is prepared to accept that the staying power and ambition of working class children varies from one part of the country to another and is at its lowest in just those areas where grammar school places are in short supply. This is improbable to say the least.

If the eight-year tests, rather than the eleven-year tests, are taken as the criterion of ability, the manual working class children are at a considerably greater disadvantage.

It was [previously] estimated that if all children were to be given the opportunities enjoyed by the upper middle class children of similar ability at eleven, the provision of grammar school places would have to be increased from 21 per cent to 27 per cent. When ability is measured by the eight-year tests, it may be estimated in the same way that the provision of places would have to be increased to 33 per cent.

How realistic are these figures? In the long run we shall have to judge this by seeing what happens to children in the grammar schools of Wales and the South-West, where the intake is already at this high level.

But an immediate indication of whether this estimate is unrealistic is given by the teachers' views on their pupils' ability to profit from a grammar school type of education; these fit closely with the estimates which were made on the basis of performance in the eleven-year tests. In the upper manual working class, for example, the teachers say that 28 per cent of the children should go to grammar school as compared with 26 per cent estimated from the results of the tests. In the lower manual working class the equivalent figures are 17 per cent and 18 per cent. The close correspondence between the views of the teachers and the estimates based on the eleven-year tests are echoed by the aspirations of the parents. Thirty per cent of the upper manual working class parents and 22 per cent of the lower manual working class parents hope that their children will go to grammar schools and stay there until they are seventeen at least. The evidence of this study, then, points to there being a shortage of grammar school places. Owing to this, able working children with parents who are willing to let them profit from a grammar school education are being deprived of the opportunity.

One other attribute of the parents should be discussed here—their age. This has a practical value in interpreting attitudes to education. Each year more parents encourage their children to stay on at school after fifteen. Does this reflect the attitude of the younger parents who, having themselves stayed on at school, are more ambitious for their children; or is it explained by more general influences? Perhaps parents of all ages are becoming more aware of the value of education in modern society, or perhaps more of them today can allow their children to stay on at school after fifteen. Some of the parents in this study were at school in the first world war and others in the second, so that there are in the same sample widely separated generations. Yet no consistent differences are found. In the upper middle classes the oldest fathers would keep their children longest at school, in the other classes the youngest would do so. In no instance was there on the average a difference of more than three months between the views of the oldest and youngest parents. It seems that similar attitudes to education are shown by parents of all ages, and that the secular trend towards later school-leaving is a result of a general change affecting all parents and not only the younger ones.

. . . . .

[How far is the performance of children in the tests and in the secondary selection examination] influenced by the attitudes of their parents, and the encouragement they receive at home?

A rough measure of the mothers' educational aspirations [may be obtained] by separating those who wished their children to go to grammar schools and stay there until they were more than sixteen years old, from those who were educationally less ambitious. The mothers' attitudes, even when measured in this rough way, have an important influence on their children's chances of getting grammar school places. But parents may give support and encouragement to their children even though they realise that they are not clever enough to stand a chance of getting a place in a grammar school. A more generally applicable measure of educational interest is needed, which moreover, takes account of the attitudes of both parents and not of the mother alone.

The middle class parents take more interest in their children's progress at school than the manual working class parents do, and they become relatively more interested as their children grow older. They visit the schools more frequently to find out how their children are getting on with their work, and when they do so are more likely to ask to see the Head as well as the class teacher, whereas the manual working class parents are usually content to see the class teacher only. But the most striking difference is that many middle class fathers visit the schools to discuss their children's progress whereas manual working class fathers seldom do so. (Thirty-two per cent of middle class fathers visit the schools, but only 12 per cent of manual working class fathers.) The teachers' contacts with the working class families are largely through the mothers, and this may explain why they become relatively less frequent as the children get older, whereas with the middle classes they become more frequent. The working class mothers have a particular interest in seeing how their children settle in when they first go to school, but may feel diffident about discussing their educational progress with the teachers at a later stage; and it seems either that their husbands are not prepared to take on this responsibility, or that they are unable to do so owing to the difficulty of taking time off work to visit the schools.

The parents who make frequent visits to the schools and are seen by the teachers as very interested in their children's education are also outstanding in the use they make of the available medical services. They seldom fail to bring their children to the child welfare centres or have them immunised against diphtheria and other diseases and they are regarded by the health visitors as giving a high standard of care to their children and homes. Their children benefit not only from the support and encouragement they get in their school work but also from the excellent personal and medical care they enjoy at home.

In contrast, the parents who seldom visit the schools and seem to the teachers to be uninterested in their children's progress make little use of the available medical services, often fail to take their children to the welfare centres or to have them immunised and, according to the health visitors, often neglect their homes and give their children low standards of care. There is a greater amount of illness and school absence among their children, whose work suffers to some extent from this as well as from their parents' lack of interest in their educational progress. Perhaps this extra burden of illness explains why these parents worry about their children's health and behaviour more than the other parents. These worries may be partly justified, but one carries away a picture of a group of mothers who are worrying about their children without taking the steps necessary to put things right.

In this study, the level of the parents' interest in their children's work was partly based on comments made by the class teachers at the end of the first and at the end of the fourth primary school year, and partly on the records of the number of times each parent visited the schools to discuss their child's progress with the Head or class teacher. Parents are said to show a 'high level of interest' if the teachers regarded them throughout the primary school period as very interested in their children's work and if they had also taken the opportunity to visit the primary schools at least once a year to discuss their children's progress. They show a 'fair level of interest' if they fall short on one of these counts, and a 'low level of interest' if they fall short on more than one.

These three groups of parents differ sharply in their educational aspirations—for example, in their views on school leaving and their hopes that their children will get grammar school places. On the average, the children in these three groups are also of widely different ability and . . . have very different attitudes to their studies; moreover they are numerous enough for satisfactory statistical comparisons to be made among the four social classes. Although this grading gives only a crude picture of the level of the parents' interest, it has been a great aid to understanding the part played in primary school education by the support and encouragement children receive from their homes.

The parents who are most interested in their children's education come predominantly from the middle classes, and those who are least interested from the manual working classes. Within each social class, however, the parents who give their children the most encouragement in their school work also give them the best care in infancy. The manual working class parents show this more strongly than the middle class parents; if they show a high level of interest in their children's school work, then their standards of care and their use of the services are also high, and they have middle class standards too in their views on the school leaving age and in their expectations of grammar school awards.

An eight-year-old child will be greatly influenced, one would imagine, by the attitude of his parents to his school work. His own attitude to his work will be moulded by theirs and, if they are ambitious for his success, he will have the further advantage of home tuition in reading and probably other subjects. Even in the early years at the primary school his test performance will show the effects of these pressures which, as he grows older and the 11+ examination approaches, are likely to increase in intensity. It is expected, then, that the parents' attitudes will have a considerable effect on the performance of children at eight years and an even greater effect on the performance of the eleven-year-olds. This is borne out by the results of this survey.

At both eight and eleven years, but particularly at eleven, the highest average scores in the tests are made by the children whose parents are the most interested in their education and the lowest by those whose parents are the least interested. This is partly a social class effect stemming from the large proportion of upper middle class children among the former and of manual working class children among the latter. But the relation between the children's scores and their parents' attitudes persists within each social class. It is less marked in the middle classes than in the manual working classes, but is substantial in both and cannot be explained away in terms of social selection alone. In the upper middle class, for instance, the children of very interested parents make scores that are 3.7 points higher on the average than those made by the children of uninterested parents. In the lower manual working class they make scores that are 9.2 points higher.

The children who are encouraged in their studies by their parents do better in each type of test, in picture intelligence tests as well as in those of reading, vocabulary and arithmetic. Their advantage is, however, less in the tests which are given pictorially or in diagrammmatic form. Those with very interested parents make higher scores at both eight and eleven years in the tests of school subjects than they do in the picture or non-verbal intelligence tests. At each age they may be considered as being on the average 'over-achievers', and by the same criterion, the children of uninterested parents may be considered 'under-achievers'.

The children whose parents show a high level of interest not only make higher average scores in the tests at eight and eleven years, but also improve the level of their performance between these ages so that they pull ahead. After allowing for the influence of social class, the children whose parents show a high level of interest improve their scores by an average of 1.06 points, and those whose parents show an average interest improve by 0.29 points, and those whose parents show little interest deteriorate by 0.18 points. The increasing advantage of the children with interested parents cannot be explained by the changes that were made in the types of test used at eight and eleven because it is as marked in the reading and vocabulary tests as in the combined test scores.

The children with interested parents pull ahead of the rest whatever their initial starting ability, as is seen in Table 3.

*Table 3. Lower Manual Working Class Children*

| | LEVEL OF PARENTS' INTEREST | | |
|---|---|---|---|
| LEVEL OF MEASURED ABILITY AT EIGHT | HIGH CHANGE IN SCORE 8–11 YEARS | AVERAGE CHANGE IN SCORE 8–11 YEARS | LOW CHANGE IN SCORE 8–11 YEARS |
| 40 or less | * | +2.07 | +0.58 |
| 41–45 | * | +0.79 | −0.42 |
| 46–50 | * | +2.17 | −0.71 |
| 51–55 | +0.60 | −0.63 | −0.96 |
| 56–60 | +1.50 | −1.65 | −3.16 |
| 61 and over | −1.36 | −4.00 | −5.71 |

* Fewer than 10 children in these groups.

+ = improved     − = deteriorated

The children who are encouraged in their work by their parents are, it seems, at an advantage both in the relatively high scores they make in the tests and in the way they improve their scores between eight and eleven years. How far is this because these children are stimulated by their parents? Could it not equally well be explained by saying that the interested parents are themselves likely to be relatively successful in life and so in a position to live in good homes and to send their children to the best schools? May not the advantages enjoyed by their children stem mainly from the better teaching they get in school and from the generally good environment in which they live? A firm answer to the questions is given in Table 4, . . . where the overlapping effects of standard of home, size of family and academic record of the school, on test performance are removed, leaving a series of adjusted average test scores which show the residual influence of parents' interest on measured ability. After these adjustments, the advantage of the children with interested parents is somewhat reduced but still considerable.

*Table 4. 8- and 11-Year Test Scores (Adjusted Means)*

|  | BOYS | | GIRLS | |
|---|---|---|---|---|
|  | 8-YRS. | 11-YRS. | 8-YRS. | 11-YRS. |
| Middle class: | | | | |
| Interested parents | 56.0 | 57.5 | 56.2 | 57.4 |
| Less interested parents | 52.7 | 53.9 | 53.3 | 53.5 |
| *Difference* | 3.3 | 3.6 | 2.9 | 3.9 |
| Manual working class: | | | | |
| Interested parents | 51.3 | 51.3 | 52.0 | 52.6 |
| Less interested parents | 47.9 | 47.2 | 48.4 | 47.7 |
| *Difference* | 3.4 | 4.1 | 3.6 | 4.9 |

In each social class, children have a considerable advantage in the eight-year tests if their parents take an interest in their school work, and an even greater advantage at eleven. The influence of the level of the parents' interest on test performance is greater than that of any of the other three factors—size of family, standard of home, and academic record of the school—which are included in this analysis, and it becomes increasingly important as the children grow older. It is among the girls especially that this effect is seen. Among the working class boys, parents' interest is only slightly more important at eleven than at eight, whereas among the middle class boys it even shows a relative decline: the test performance at eleven is then correspondingly more affected by the type of school they attend and the number of brothers and sisters they have.

As one would expect from their test scores, children do relatively well in the secondary selection examinations if their parents take much interest in their work and relatively badly if they take little interest. This difference is most marked in the manual working classes, where 40 per cent of the former and only 10 per cent of the latter go to grammar schools. The teachers, though more optimistic than the results of the 11+ examinations justify, take a similar view and consider that 59 per cent of the manual working class children are suitable for grammar schools if their parents are interested, and only 15 per cent if they are uninterested. In the middle classes also the teachers' views show a similar agreement with the results of secondary school selection and the level of the parents' interest.

The children with parents who are interested in their work do well in the secondary selection examinations and are favourably rated by their teachers largely because they are of superior measured ability at eleven. Once this factor is allowed for, they still have a slight additional advantage in the examinations; those with very interested parents get 10 per cent more places than we would expect, whereas those with uninterested parents get 7 per cent fewer. It is however the children at the borderline of the level of ability needed for grammar school entrance, who get substantially more grammar school places if their parents are interested in their work; they get 19 per cent more places than expected whereas those with uninterested parents get 14 per cent fewer.

The influence of the parents on their children's chances in the secondary selection examinations is better shown when the children are grouped by the wishes their parents expressed when they were ten years old, wishes for the type of school they should go to, and how long they should stay there. Among children of measured ability between 55 and 60, i.e., those who are at the borderline for grammar school entry, those whose mothers wish them to go to grammar school and stay there till seventeen at least get 23 per cent more places than expected, those whose mothers are doubtful get 24 per cent fewer places and those who expect to go to a secondary modern school and leave before seventeen get 69 per cent fewer places than expected. This is hardly surprising, for the school interest score is an attempt to measure the level of support and encouragement which will help children of widely different ability to take an interest in their studies and use their capabilities as far as they can, whereas the wishes parents expressed for the type of school their children should go to are likely to indicate the pressures that may have been used to stimulate children of above average ability to get a valued prize.

## Suggestions for Further Reading

FLANN CAMPBELL, *Eleven-Plus and All That* (London: Watts, 1956). An underrated historical and sociological account of secondary school selection in London, this study provides indispensable background material with which to read *The Home and the School*.

JEAN FLOUD, A. H. HALSEY, and F. M. MARTIN, *Social Class and Educational Opportunity* (London: Heinemann, 1956). This is a classic study of the influence of social class on educational opportunity in two areas in Britain (southwest Hertfordshire and Middlesborough).

DAVID V. GLASS, ed., *Social Mobility in Britain* (London: Routledge and Kegan Paul, 1954). Chapter V by Jean Floud, Chapter VI by Hilde Himmelweit, and Chapter VII by F. M. Martin deal with various aspects of educational selection in Britain. Chapter X by J. R. Hall and D. V. Glass links education with social mobility.

A. H. HALSEY, JEAN FLOUD, and C. A. ANDERSON, eds., *Education, Economy and Society* (Glencoe, Ill.: Free Press, 1963). A reader in the sociology of education, all six sections contain valuable material reprinted from studies of various aspects of British education which is comparable with the American and other material also contained in the volume.

BRIAN JACKSON and DENNIS MARSDEN, *Education and the Working Class* (London: Routledge and Kegan Paul, 1962). This impressionistic study of 88 working-class and 10 middle-class children from the North of England was conducted by the Institute of Community Studies. It is useful for filling out some of the themes touched on briefly in *The Home and the School*.

# ⅋Infant Care in an Urban Community

JOHN AND ELIZABETH NEWSON

*Sociologists have always been impressed by the very evident fact that the members of different social groups vary in the way they perceive the world around them and their own place in it. In particular they have sought to explain the marked differences between the middle and the working classes in this respect by referring to differential mortality and occupational mobility rates, to variations in the life chances and life experiences of the various social classes. At this point the interest of the sociologist converges toward that of those social psychologists who, inspired by the work of the Freudians, have been attempting to develop a theory of basic personality structure. Briefly, this theory holds that how people see the world depends on their personalities, that although modifiable by experience throughout a lifetime all personalities have a basic core which is laid down in early childhood, and that many people within a given culture will have similar basic personality structures because they are subjected to almost identical child-rearing practices. What has been lacking to complete this convergence has been satisfactory data on the extent to which mothers and fathers in the same social class rear their children in the light of the same set of beliefs about the correct way to behave as parents; and, more important, equally lacking has been reliable information on the differences between parents of the middle and working classes in these respects.*

*The following selection provides the beginning of an attack on the problem. Over a period of two years, 709 mothers in Nottingham, the eighth largest city in England, were interviewed by health visitors and by staff of the University of Nottingham to find out how they actually handled their one-year-old babies, irrespective of how they were told to handle them, and how as a matter of fact their babies normally responded. The interviewing was conducted at home on a questionnaire compiled by the Newsons which was in part highly structured and in part almost completely open-ended. Portable tape recorders were used to record the mothers' own words if necessary. The aim was the very modest one of merely attempting to estimate the extent of difference in infant care in an urban setting.*

*Although the authors are aware of the relevance of their findings for a thorough attack on the basic personality problem, they regard their work as preliminary only. Much more data on later years of life and on other groups is required before the results can be put to good use. Nevertheless, as they themselves say, "We have to start somewhere. The survey is itself only a part of the general trend towards a psychological ecology in which psychological problems are studied less in the laboratories and the clinics and to a far greater extent in the natural habitat of the human animal."*

Infant Care in an Urban Community *reports work which was begun in 1959. Fortunately the Newsons were able to continue their researches beyond the first year of life. A second study of 275 of the original children has been completed,[1] and a further survey with the sample increased to 700 is at present under way. It is hoped that the children will be studied longitudinally at least until they leave school. In this way it may be expected that the final outcome will prove to be as much a contribution to sociology as to psychology.*

SOURCE: John and Elizabeth Newson, *Infant Care in an Urban Community*, Chapters 12 and 13 (pp. 176–201). Copyright © 1963 by George Allen and Unwin. Reprinted by permission.
[1] John and Elizabeth Newson, *Four Years Old in an Urban Community* (London: Allen and Unwin, 1968).

The problem of discipline, in the sense of the prevention of 'naughtiness' and the promotion of 'goodness', has hardly yet begun to assume any importance for the parents of the twelve-months-old baby; nevertheless, the infant's behaviour, even in the first few months, is frequently evaluated in moral terms. Thus, although babies are rarely described as bad or wicked, difficult babies who demand a lot of attention often seem to be regarded as little tyrants deliberately trying to get the upper hand in a struggle for power ('she's on the fiendish side', as one mother said), while easy, passive babies are held up as models of perfection and natural goodness.

Together with this assumption of good or bad intent in small babies goes the theory, sometimes explicitly stated, sometimes merely implied, that early and correct 'habit training' is of considerable importance as a foundation for later character building; and, conversely, that the wrong sort of training in infancy may permanently mar or spoil the child's character. Criticism of a parent's methods of upbringing frequently revolves round this central idea of the spoilt child; and this applies not only to neighbour's criticism of neighbour, or a woman's of her sister, but also to that inter-class criticism which is directed by the member of one social class against the stereotype of another. Thus the middle-class mother may have an idea of the 'spoilt' working-class child, continually indulged with sugared dummy [pacifier], sticky sweets and chips; the working-class woman sees the 'spoilt' middle-class child getting away with wilfulness and 'temper' which a good unselfconscious slap would soon cure. And here at once it becomes apparent that the idea of spoiling may mean different things to different mothers. For some, its chief ingredient is material indulgence: the child is too often given the sweets, the rich food, the toys that he demands; for others, it is an indulgence of the child's self-esteem: he is allowed to be 'cheeky' or 'cocky', he 'answers back', he demands and receives his mother's attention—in short, he 'needs to be taken down a peg'. Some mothers are criticized for spoiling their children by letting them leave food on their plate, or eat cake before bread and butter, or choose their own bedtime; others, for sparing the rod and thus failing in their traditional parental duty. Spoiling may be taken by one to mean that the parents exercise all too little control and supervision over the child; by another, that they are over-protective of him and control him so closely that he expects everything to be done for him and is unable to develop his own spirit of independence.

It is clear that two separate factors are involved in the notion of spoiling: firstly, the *type of behaviour* which, unchecked, denotes a spoilt child; secondly, the *method of checking or correcting* which, if used, would presumably have prevented his becoming spoilt. We need to have these two issues in mind when we investigate class differences in the moral attitudes expressed by mothers in their handling of their children. On the first issue, are there reliable class differences in the kind of behaviour which is considered 'naughty'? that is to say, do parents in different social class groups attach importance to different aspects of child training? If they do, then it is probable that the notion of the spoilt child will vary from class to class as each group labels as 'spoiling' any failure to check the special forms of behaviour of which it disapproves; and it may even happen that behaviour considered 'spoilt', 'naughty' or 'rude' by one class may be valued by the members of another class for its 'independence', 'character' or 'grownup-ness'. On the second issue, do social classes differ in the means parents employ—the pressures they bring to bear, the punishments they use and the persistence with which sanctions are enforced—as they attempt to make the child conform to whatever standards they consider desirable?

There appear to be fairly clear class differences in parents' attitudes towards indulging a baby in his desire to suck, once this is no longer important as the primary means of taking nourishment. In comparison with working-class mothers, middle-class women often seem to have a deep-seated objection to the idea of allowing a child to continue with the infantile practice of sucking for mere pleasure during the second year of life. For some reason, the bottle is totally unacceptable as a mere drinking-vessel for the older toddler: it seems to have emotional overtones for the middle-class woman which make her regard weaning to the cup as a matter of great importance, and failure to wean [2] as something to worry about. As the child nears his first birthday, the middle-class mother begins to feel that she really must make a special effort to separate him from his beloved bottle; and, if the dummy has been allowed at all, she will be setting limits to that 'bad habit' too: 'Once he's finished teething, I shall really have to do something about it'.

On the other hand, the *means* by which children, of any class, are discouraged from seeking oral gratification are not, in general, severe, especially when compared with the methods which have been advised in the past. Rarely, it seems, does the baby meet with an absolute refusal to his demands to continue sucking; the mother will hide the bottle or dummy in the hope that the child will forget about it, but she will not actually get rid of it. She may attempt to provide attractive alternatives—a special new drinking-cup, perhaps, or playthings which she hopes the baby will find preferable to the dummy. There seems to be no question nowadays that the mother should insist on the child's giving up the bottle against his will: even where she is determined to wean him, the process tends to be one of gentle discouragement, distraction and very gradual change, and the firmness that used to be so strongly advocated has quite disappeared. This leniency in the method of weaning from bottle or dummy seems to apply in all occupational groups; the main difference between classes is simply that the middle-class mother starts the process earlier. We saw the working of this principle particularly clearly in the homes of those working-class mothers who were beginning to think of breaking the dummy habit (it will be remembered that middle-class dummies are kept well hidden from callers). Often the dummy would be pointed out to the interviewer, high on the mantelpiece where the baby could not see it, but ready for immediate use if necessary: 'I keep it up there so she'll not think about it, like. But I wouldn't stop her off it, not if she wanted it. If she cries for it, I'll give it her'. So the older toddler may be ridiculed, scolded, even smacked for still sucking a dummy; but it doesn't seem to occur to

[2] By 'failing to wean' we imply here only that the child is still using a bottle for drinking purposes, not that he has failed to take solids.

the mother simply to throw the dummy away and refuse to replace it: that would be cruel. Sometimes the mother will have 'managed without' a dummy for the latest baby, having experienced difficulty in breaking an earlier sibling of the habit; here again, it is the long process of relatively lenient discouragement that she is consciously avoiding—a short, sharp break is simply not entertained as a possibility.

Returning, then, to our analysis of 'spoiling', in this area of upbringing we find agreement between social classes on the means by which training should proceed but some disagreement on what in fact constitutes the spoilt child. Both middle- and working-class mothers do their best to make weaning as easy and pleasant as possible; but the middle-class woman already begins to feel that she is spoiling her baby by allowing him the bottle beyond his first birthday. For the middle-class mother, then, the situation is anomalous: she has rather puritanical expectations of what the baby *should* be doing, but she is not prepared to back them up with a firm enforcement of discipline; in other words, she has rejected the strict, Truby King-inspired regime of her own mother's day, but still hankers after the well-behaved baby which, ideally speaking, was its product. The result is that she is apt to feel guilty and ashamed of behaviour which the working-class woman accepts as natural and reasonable.

The general trend against imposing one's will too forcibly upon the baby has interesting repercussions in the mothers' attitudes to thumb-sucking as opposed to dummy-sucking. Only a very small proportion of our sample (8½ per cent) sucked their thumbs at twelve months, probably because most of them had more satisfying alternatives; the great majority were middle-class babies. Where thumb-sucking did occur, however, it was accepted by middle-class mothers as a lesser evil,[3] in the small baby even a pretty sight, and at least a 'natural' comfort rather than an artificial one; mainly, however, because they had no choice, since thumb-sucking cannot be stopped except by rather forceful and unpleasant means which are

[3] Despite what seems to be the general medical view that dummies, provided they are not sugar-dipped, do less harm to the teeth than thumb-sucking.

no longer tolerated: one cannot put the thumb on the mantelpiece in the hope that the child will forget it!

## Bedtime and Wakefulness

Mothers of different social classes also seem to diverge in their opinions of how far soothing the child to sleep is permissible before he is in danger of becoming spoilt. There seems to be a strong middle-class feeling that babies should learn early to go to sleep at a 'reasonable' hour without help and without making a fuss. Ideally, the baby is tucked up in his cot at the appropriate time, and left without distraction or social companionship to get in with the business of going to sleep. In line with their general tendency to discourage sucking at this age, middle-class mothers are much less likely than working-class mothers to allow their children the solace of a bottle or dummy with which to fall asleep.

Middle-class mothers also expect their children to settle for the night somewhat earlier than do working-class mothers. This is shown by the times at which the children had in fact been put to bed on the evening preceding the interview: as before, those for whom bedtime

*Table 1.[4] Early and Late Bedtimes of One-year-olds, Analysed by Social Class*

|  | I AND II | III WC | III MAN | IV | V | ALL CLASSES |
|---|---|---|---|---|---|---|
| Normal bedtime at or before 6.30 p.m. | % | % | % | % | % | % |
|  | 47 | 31 | 29 | 24 | 31 | 31 |
| Normal bedtime at or after 8.0 p.m. | 7 | 12 | 20 | 23 | 26 | 18 |

[4] In this and subsequent Tables, the class references should be interpreted as follows: I and II *Professional and managerial*, III W.C. *White collar*, III Man *skilled manual*, IV *Semi-skilled*, V *Unskilled*. These references are to the occupations of the husbands of the mothers interviewed.

was abnormal on that day have been excluded. Table 1 shows the proportions of babies in the different social classes whose normal bedtimes were before 6.30 p.m. or after 8.0 p.m. Here professional families differ from the rest in the proportion of babies who are settled to sleep early; while the percentage of mothers allowing a relatively late bedtime increases fairly steadily as we descend the class scale, and the overall difference between classes is again significant.

That middle-class babies are much more likely to be put to sleep in a room alone is shown in Table 2. These proportions could, of

*Table 2. Children Sleeping in a Room Alone, Analysed by Social Class*

| I AND II | III WC | III MAN | IV | V | ALL CLASSES |
|---|---|---|---|---|---|
| 54% | 42% | 20% | 18% | 3% | 26% |

course, be attributed entirely to the fact that middle-class families enjoy standards of accommodation which make it possible to give the baby a room to himself, while working-class families are far less likely to be able to do so. Middle-class mothers do seem to show greater concern over this question, however, and we found indications that the availability of bedroom space was not the only consideration involved. [There is a] . . . convenience in being able to reach out of bed to comfort the restless infant in the cot alongside; . . . where the dummy or bottle is used, the advantages of the baby sleeping in the parents' room are even greater, since teat can be popped in mouth at his first stirring and he may thus be soothed back to sleep before he is actually awake. The child in a separate room, on the other hand, will probably be fully awake before his parents hear him, and will be all the more difficult to get back to sleep. Thus, unless middle-class parents have special reasons for being prepared to endure the discomfort of getting up in the night—and it may, of course, be true that they do worry more than working-class parents about the psychological consequences of the baby witnessing the sexual act—the belief that a child of this age should have a room to himself implies an act of faith that if he has been properly trained in good sleeping habits (if he has not been spoilt, that is to say) he will not in fact demand attention at night. An act of faith: for, at this age at least, there are no consistent or significant differences between classes in the proportions of children who actually do wake during the night.

Despite the middle-class emphasis on 'good' sleeping habits, it would be wrong to assume that middle-class mothers are especially harsh in the way in which they deal with the problem of settling the baby at bedtime or of getting him back to sleep if he does wake. They are, of course, less likely than working-class mothers to use bottle or dummy during the night; nor are they so willing to take the baby into their own bed to comfort him. But the middle-class baby is not more often left to cry than the working-class child, nor for longer periods; again, expectations may be higher, but treatment of the baby is not in practice any more strict.

It seems probable that the middle-class insistence upon getting the children off to bed early is partly a reflection of other social habits associated with class. One important factor must be the 'high tea'. For many working-class families this will be the main meal of the day, the time when the whole family meets round the table; geared to the homecoming of the 'mester', it will probably take place at about 6.0 to 6.30 p.m. This means that what by middle-class mothers is thought of as the 'proper' bedtime for a baby or toddler falls right in the middle of the period needed for the preparation and consumption of high tea. Thus the baby must either be put to bed before his father comes home or wait until after tea; and the latter seems to be more usual, perhaps partly because 'her daddy likes to have that little time with her, it's the only chance he really gets of seeing her during the week'. The high tea habit is, of course, spreading rapidly, not only from the north of England to the south, but also from working to middle class;[5] but this would seem to be a change to which there is some resistance in middle-class families

[5] W. S. Crawford, Ltd., Market Research Division: *The Foods We Eat* (Cassell, 1958).

until the children are of school age: our own (non-statistical) observations are that a five o'clock tea for small children is the norm, particularly in families at the professional level. This is followed by father's return home and a short playtime, after which the children are packed off to bed and the parents are free to enjoy their evening meal together. For many middle-class mothers this is a time to be hotly defended against any incursion from the rest of the family: the evening is looked forward to throughout the day as a time for relaxation in the company of husband and perhaps other adults. People no longer dress for dinner, but middle-class women cherish the more formal pleasures of polite conversation about adult affairs in a more leisured and sophisticated atmosphere than is possible in the daytime clamour of children and chores.

## Toilet Training

When we come to analyse class attitudes to toilet training as evidenced by the mothers' efforts to teach their babies the use of the potty, we find that Class V mothers again show a very marked divergence from the rest of the population. The first difference is that so many of them do *not* in fact make any such effort at this stage; more unexpected is the finding that those who do attempt toilet training report such a very high comparative rate of failure. The figures in Table 3 show, in the first place, that the proportion of unskilled workers' wives who at the child's first birthday had not yet attempted potty training is significantly greater than the proportions in other social classes; and in the second place that, even when all these late-training mothers are excluded, the proportion in Class V whose babies had 'never used the potty for wetting' is almost double the proportions in other classes. It appears, then, that as we move down the social scale, and especially as we approach the lower end, mothers tend to place less emphasis on the use of the potty and the control of urination. The trend is similar to that found in other forms of habit training, except in the very big difference between Class V and the rest, which is not very easy to interpret. Some

*Table 3. Proportions of Mothers Who at 12 Months had not yet Started Toilet Training; and, of Babies Whose Training had Started, Proportions Who had never yet used the Potty for Wetting: Analysed by Social Class*

|  | I AND II | III WC | III MAN | IV | V | ALL CLASSES |
|---|---|---|---|---|---|---|
| Training not yet | % | % | % | % | % | % |
| started | 12 | 16 | 17 | 13 | 32 | 17 |
| Of those started, percentage | | | | | | |
| never successful | 36 | 38 | 46 | 42 | 79 | 46 |

mothers have a very casual attitude towards wetting, and allow the child to make puddles where he pleases and to spend much of the day bare-bottomed in order to save washing; but this seems to be an aspect of the individual mother's personality rather than of class; we have encountered it in every type of home, and in general it is a typical behaviour, rather disapproved of by the majority. In any case, working-class modesty seems to preclude such an explanation; in answer to our question on masturbation, it was working-class mothers in particular who emphasized the importance of keeping the child well covered below the waist.

Nor is it true that mothers in Class V all have the latest washing machines on hire purchase, and can therefore afford to be casual over toilet training. The middle-class belief that the majority of working-class mothers are more lavishly equipped than themselves with television sets and washing machines has been disproved before; our own figures for the possession of washing machines are shown in Table 4. Of course, the fact that a mother is casual in her attitude to toilet training does not necessarily mean that she has immense quantities of nappies to wash; we did not inquire into the number of times any given child's nappy was changed, but observation suggests that many children spend much of their time encased in sodden nappies inside the universal plastic pants.

Table 4. Social Class and Ownership of Washing Machines

| | I AND II | III WC | III MAN | IV | V | ALL CLASSES |
|---|---|---|---|---|---|---|
| Mothers with washing machines | 72% | 61% | 45% | 51% | 26% | 48% |

Equally difficult to understand is the very noticeable failure of Class V mothers to persuade their infants to use the potty. The criterion here is a very low one: simply that the baby occasionally uses or has used the potty for wetting. If this is largely a matter of luck at this age, why are so many Class V mothers unlucky? If there is an element of skill or patience involved, of course, it may be that Class V mothers are less persistent in their attempts to train the child; on the evidence of those few mothers whose children were more or less trained by twelve months, a good deal of time and attention must be given to the job, and perhaps Class V mothers, with less sense of urgency about the whole business of toilet training, are unwilling to make the necessary effort at this stage. One other explanation, or partial explanation, is possible: that Class V mothers, because of their casual attitude towards toilet training, are less concerned to make a good impression and are therefore more willing to admit any failure to achieve results: while other classes, for whom the affair has greater significance, find failure unpalatable and so give more optimistic answers.

In bowel training, as distinct from training for dryness, no class differences can be shown for success or failure. For obvious aesthetic reasons, 'getting him clean' tends to be taken somewhat more seriously even by the most casual mothers; and from a practical point of view it is probably easier to 'catch' a bowel motion, since the child usually gives some involuntary warning—grunting, flushing or some other individual symptom or symptoms which soon become familiar to his mother. In Nottingham, however, we found a widespread working-class habit of holding the child out over newspaper for this purpose; and it may be that where this is done bowel training tends to become divorced from general training in the use of the pot.

Where toilet training has already been started, some mothers back up regular potty sessions with a smack for non-performance or, especially, for performance in the wrong place; . . . the child is particularly likely to get smacked if he annoys the mother by wetting or soiling his nappy immediately after a fruitless interlude on the pot. There seem to be class differences in the use of smacking in this situation. We did not ask the direct question 'do you smack him for wetting his nappy?' and we have no statistical evidence on this point; but it was clear that spontaneous mention of smacking for this sort of 'naughtiness' was far more likely to be made by the working-class mother. Middle-class mothers, even those who approved of smacking in general, almost never mentioned it in connection with potty training. One had the impression that the middle-class mother who, tried beyond her endurance, did smack for wetting in the wrong place would be ashamed of her action; whereas a fair number of working-class mothers used this method as a matter of course.

## Attitudes to Genital Play

While mothers in every class showed some embarrassment in talking about masturbation, we found very clear class differences in whether the child was checked when he tried to 'play with himself'. The picture here is somewhat confused by the fact that we do not know how many of the mothers who denied genital play in their children were in fact doing so because they preferred not to discuss the subject. However, the reported incidence of masturbation did not show any consistent class differences; this means that, if some mothers do hide this behaviour out of embarrassment, the proportion doing so is fairly constant throughout the population, since we may presumably assume that the actual incidence of attempted masturbation does not vary from class to class, in babies at any rate. But, whatever doubts one may have as to the frankness of some mothers about what the baby does, the class trend in the mothers' behaviour in response to masturbation is very marked indeed. Nearly all Class V mothers try to stop the child touching or playing with his genitals at this age; only a quarter of professional men's wives do so, and it is interesting to notice that there is a considerable difference between their attitude and that of the wives of other white-collar workers.'

*Table 5. Of Mothers Who Report Genital Play in their Children, Proportions Who Attempt to Prevent its Occurrence; Analysed by Social Class*

|  | I AND II | III WC | III MAN | IV | V |
|---|---|---|---|---|---|
| Mother checks genital play | 25% | 50% | 57% | 69% | 93% |

We can suggest two factors which contribute to this trend. One is the working-class sense of modesty: in breast feeding, in toilet training, in the father's care of his small daughter, this squeamishness about the exposure of the body appears as an exclusively working-class feeling; it is only in the actual handling of the genitals that a few middle-class mothers begin to impose sanctions at this age, and even here they are in a minority for their class. The second factor is probably the influence of the baby books. Genital play is a subject on which the books seem to be united in advising that it is natural behaviour for a small child and that nothing need be done about it; the older child may be distracted and 'care must be taken to fill their lives with interest and to give them plenty of affection (but) the habit itself should be ignored'.[6] That standard manuals of baby care should take this line is of course a comparatively recent development, in terms of generations of children: a comparison of two editions of *The Mothercraft Manual* illustrates the shift in advice. The quotation above appears in the 1954 edition, and ends: 'Parents need no longer look upon it as a vice'; the 1928 edition, while advising distraction rather than scolding for the older child,

[6] Mabel Liddiard: *The Mothercraft Manual,* 12th edition (Churchill, 1954).

for fear that he should learn to do it secretly, is very definite that preventive measures should be taken where the baby is concerned:

'. . . The great thing is to recognize the condition early . . . Untiring zeal on the part of the mother or nurse is the only cure; it may be necessary to put the legs in splints before putting the child to bed. He must never be left in such a position that he can carry on the habit, he must be made to forget it; this sometimes takes three months, or longer in the worst cases. . . . This habit, if left unchecked, may develop into a serious vice. The child's moral nature becomes perverted; one such child has been known to upset a whole school. The important thing is to detect the habit in infancy, when it is much easier to stop than in later years.'

If we are correct in believing that the correlation between class trends in the use of reference books and in the toleration of genital play is a causal one, then one would expect that historically we should find the same sort of cross-over in class attitudes as we found in attitudes towards breast feeding: this would be shown in the middle-class mother's conscientious restriction of masturbation in the 'twenties and 'thirties, followed by an equally conscientious permissiveness in the 'fifties and 'sixties, while the working-class mother would have been relatively unaffected by book advice in either period. Having no information or class differences in the treatment of babies' genital play in the nineteen-twenties, we can only speculate.

## Temper Tantrums

How far tantrums are a necessary part of the young child's behaviour and how far they are avoidable is a matter for speculation; what seems certain is that at twelve months many children are already displaying these outbursts of rage. Some indication that they can be avoided may be given by the fact that class differences do appear in the numbers of children having 'frequent' tantrums; on the other hand, there may be other factors influencing the class trend, which is shown in Table 6. Significant differences are found between all white-collar workers and the rest, and between unskilled workers and the rest.

*Table 6. Temper Tantrums and Social Class*

|  | I AND II | III WC | III MAN | IV | V | ALL CLASSES |
|---|---|---|---|---|---|---|
| Tantrums reported as 'frequent' | 9% | 8% | 14% | 15% | 23% | 14% |

Temper tantrums in the small child seem to be his reaction to a frustrating situation which he is unable to deal with otherwise. Sometimes the source of frustration will be his own lack of skill in manipulating his material environment; more often, frustration will have been imposed upon him by some person, usually his mother. In this situation of social frustration, typically there is a clash of wills between mother and baby; either she wants him to do what he doesn't want to do—have his nappy changed, for instance—or she prevents him in doing what he does want to do.

Inevitably, in the normal everyday life of a baby there will be many opportunities for frustration, and therefore for temper tantrums. Children cannot be allowed to tear wallpaper or books, to fling cups off the table or to climb into the fire. Some mothers, in addition, cannot tolerate the noise of clanging fire-irons or the mess that a baby can get into when he tries to mop the kitchen floor or take a hand in his feeding. In general, a mother has three alternatives when a situation of this sort arises: she can give in to the baby's wish (but this may be dangerous or inexpedient); she can insist on her own course of action, possibly giving the child a smack for good measure, and risk a tantrum; or she can, while insisting that the child conforms to her will on the point at issue, so distract him by special cuddling or by drawing his attention to other attractive occupations that his frustration is reduced and a tantrum averted. In the words of [one Nottingham mother], the child is *loved* out of the situation rather than being *bullied* out of the situation. Loving and distracting, however, take time and effort, and it is easier to slap a child and then let him have his tantrum out; to judge from what they say, many mothers do in fact use slapping as a short-cut method of temporarily relaxing a child's grip or his resistant body.

In this we may find some clue to the reason for the very small number of professional-class children who have frequent tantrums at this age. This group of mothers, as we have seen, is also more inclined to manage the baby without recourse to smacking; and it may well be that non-smacking is a good indication at this age of the mother who is prepared to reject short-cut methods in favour of treatment which demands more patience on her part, but which proportionally reduces the child's tension and therefore his·need for anger and aggression. The class differences in reported incidence of tantrums cannot be entirely explained on this basis, however. We still have to account for the fact that Class III white-collar mothers, although smacking almost as often as manual workers' wives, are also rare to report frequent tantrums; in addition, there is the sudden increase in tantrums in Class V children.

Since we can presumably discount between-class constitutional differences in the children themselves [7] (and there is no reason to suppose that the more intelligent child, for instance, is any less prone to tantrums at this age), we are left with two possibilities: firstly that, aside from smacking, there may be other class differences in treatment which affect the incidence of tantrums; and, secondly, that there may be certain class factors which influence the accuracy of the mother's report. Probably both of these are involved.

Smacking is not the only short-cut method in discipline. The mother who first leaves out of account her child's wishes and then is able to ignore his furious reaction is, in the short term, saving time. A good many mothers do seem to ignore and indulge in a rather haphazard manner: a typical pattern of mother-child inter-action is shown when the baby firstly is frustrated without mitigation, then has a temper tantrum, then is slapped for the tantrum, then is given a sweet or a dummy to help him get over the slap. Completely *ad hoc* methods of this sort seem to be relatively common only among Class V families, however; skilled workers' wives

---

[7] One cannot, of course, ignore constitutional differences as a general factor in proneness to temper tantrums.

tend to be a little more consistent, and white-collar wives to deplore such treatment, and, whether they are strict or lenient, to show a greater consciousness of the total sequential pattern of their actions. This *taking thought* about the methods they use, typical of white-collar wives, is probably as important as any other factor in reducing the frequency of temper tantrums. An additional impression . . . is that Class V babies are more likely to be teased and exploited for the parents' amusement than are other babies; in Nottingham as in Bali,[8] this sort of treatment is likely to be productive of temper tantrums.

. . . . .

There remains the possibility that the mothers' reports of temper tantrums may not be strictly comparable between classes. The mother's own attitude towards angry behaviour may affect not only whether or not she is willing to admit that her child has frequent tantrums but also whether she labels such behaviour as 'temper tantrum' in the first place. It may be, for instance, that a mother who sympathizes with her child's need to display aggression as a stage in his development—typically a middle-class mother—may not think of this as 'temper', a word which for many has connotations of unreasonable wilfulness; the mother further down the social scale, who seems more often to think of her child as a small adversary, may be far more ready to talk of his temper in a critical or even half-admiring way. Similarly, the mother's report may be affected by the degree to which she values conformity at this age; the Class III white-collar mother, for instance, may feel that she is being let down by a child who shows rage, and may thus minimize the extent to which this happens.

Obviously a peaceable child is more pleasant to deal with than an angry one; and tantrums, while they may be tolerated as a developmental phase, are seldom approved of. The child who continues to have frequent tantrums is either 'spoilt' or well on the road to

[8] See Gregory Bateson and Margaret Mead: *Balinese Character: a photographic analysis* (New York Academy of Sciences, 1942).

becoming so: 'she's a bit distempered, her uncle spoils her, you see'. Twelve months is of course rather early for tantrums to be presenting a real problem; nevertheless, they already account for more than a quarter of babies' punishable offences. Preferences in the methods of dealing with tantrums once they have occurred are fairly equally divided between ignoring, punishing, and cuddling or distracting; there are no significant class differences to be found here. It is interesting that professional-class mothers, who smack less in general, smack almost as much as others when confronted with an enraged baby; although they are more skilful at taking avoiding action, aggression finally provokes aggression. Once again, perhaps, this leads us back to the concept of 'spoiling'. Though the characteristics of the 'ideal' spoilt child (if one may use such a term) may vary from class to class, the fear lest one's child should appear spoilt seems almost universal; and as the child grows older the temper tantrum is the plainest and most shaming symptom of all.

## Suggestions for Further Reading

J. W. B. DOUGLAS and J. M. BLOMFIELD, *Children under Five* (London: Allen and Unwin, 1958). The second of the three studies by Douglas, this provides some interesting comparisons with the Nottingham study made by the Newsons, because although it is not so detailed it has some material on health visitors' assessments of the quality of maternal care in the homes of the different social classes they visited (ch. VII).

MADELEINE KERR, *The People of Ship Street* (London: Routledge and Kegan Paul, 1958). A study of the households on a number of streets in the slum district of Liverpool, this book emphasizes the role of the mother in the family and hence concentrates rather more on family relationships generally than is the case with *Infant Care in an Urban Community*.

JOSEPHINE KLEIN, *Samples from English Cultures* (London: Routledge and Kegan Paul, 1965). Volume II of this book deals with child-rearing practices taken from a large number of studies. It is particularly valuable for pointing up the gaps in knowledge in this area where further research is required.

JOHN AND ELIZABETH NEWSON, "Cultural Aspects of Child Rearing in the English-Speaking World," in J. L. Rivoire and A. H. Kidd, eds., *Handbook of Infant Development* (Chicago: Aldine Press, 1966). This article examines notions about child-rearing and actual practices in terms of their sociological implications and usefully puts the Nottingham study into a wider perspective.

B. SPINLEY, *The Deprived and the Privileged* (London: Routledge and Kegan Paul, 1954). This study is, in addition to its material on working-class families, the main source of information on the upper middle class. Unfortunately it relies on the memories of people in their twenties as to their childhood experiences.